THE TENNIS QUIZ BOOK

THE TENNIS QUIZ BOOK

JOHN DT WHITE

First published in 2005 by
Apex Publishing Ltd
PO Box 7086, Clacton on Sea, Essex, CO15 5WN, England

www.apexpublishing.co.uk

British Library Cataloguing-in-Publication Data
A catalogue record for this book
is available from the British Library

ISBN 1-904444-45-8

Typeset in 10.5pt Times New Roman

Production Manager: Chris Cowlin

Cover Design: Andrew Macey

Printed and bound in Great Britain

This Book is dedicated to my many Friends who have always stuck by me no matter what.

In particular I just want to say THANKS to:

Anto

Big Dee

Big Jim

Billy Nolan

Brendy

Diggy

Frankie (Dodger)

Frankie McD

Joanne (aka Suzi)

JD

Keeny

McD

McG

Marty

Scrat

Sean Harmon

Stevie B

Wee Stevie

Wilson

AND

All of my Family, especially Janice, Marc & Paul.

INTRODUCTION

I have had the pleasure of writing quiz books covering football, motor racing, golf, Manchester United, Tottenham Hotspur, snooker and even the Tour de France but I must amit I really got into this book from the very beginning. Tennis in many ways has always been my second sport, although it does trail football by some distance. I will never forget watching my first Wimbledon on TV in 1975 when Arthur Ashe meditated his way to victory or Wimbledon in 1976 when the magical, mesmeric, unflappable, ice-cool superstar who is Bjorn Borg blew me away. Here was this good looking Swedish player who had the girls screaming with his chiselled looks and flowing blonde hair - God I was jealous of him! I watched in total awe as he powered his way to the first of his five consecutive Wimbledon Men's Singles titles. And if you were anything like me, you just wanted to own one of those cool red tracksuit tops he wore.

My early school holidays will always be remembered for one thing and one thing only - the Wimbledon fortnight. My friend, Anthony Farrelly, and I would sit for hours upon hours on a daily basis glued to the BBC's TV coverage of Wimbledon. Our Mums could not get us out of the house when the tennis was on. All this and Chris Evert as well. Boy was she gorgeous or what? At the end of each day's TV coverage Anthony and I would take to the street where I lived (Harper Street, Belfast) and act out that day's play on our very own Centre Court that we had drawn with chalk on the road. We had more than the occasional dispute à la McEnroe, but we always ended up mates.

Although John McEnroe finally took away my hero's crown, I quickly grew to like J P McEnroe. Here was this New York "in your face" kid who was about to take the tennis world by storm. I will always remember the outrageous outbursts on court by a certain Romanian named Ilie Nastase, but let's face it, he had nothing on Mac. It was just Mac's intense will to win that made me grow to like him and, in many ways, I am quite similar because I hate to lose, no matter what I am playing. Of course tennis has changed in so many ways since 1975. I mean some players who ended their careers as Multiple Grand Slam Winners finished their playing days in the 1970s with total prize money of around $1 million if they were lucky. Today players can win as much as $1 million in a single tournament. Amazing! And, of course, when I first watched Wimbledon most of the players used wooden rackets strung with cat gut whereas the players today have state-of-the-art weapons in their hands.

In closing, I wish to say thank you to Mark Young from the International Tennis Hall of Fame (www.tennisfame.com) and the Webmaster at www.wimbledon.org for providing some of the data and information that helped me compile a number of the questions for my book. Finally, I hope you enjoy this book and I hope, like me, it helps rekindle many fond memories of Wimbledon for you.

John DT White

MEN'S SINGLES CHAMPION - 1

ALL YOU HAVE TO DO HERE IS ASSOCIATE THE PLAYER WITH THE YEAR HE WON THE MEN'S SINGLES TITLE AT WIMBLEDON

1.	Lleyton Hewitt	1971
2.	John Newcombe	1996
3.	Jimmy Connors	2002
4.	John McEnroe	2003
5.	Bjorn Borg	2000
6.	Roger Federer	1981
7.	Goran Ivanisevic	1974
8.	Richard Krajicek	2001
9.	Jan Kodes	1980
10.	Pete Sampras	1973

LADIES' SINGLES CHAMPION - 1

ALL YOU HAVE TO DO HERE IS ASSOCIATE THE PLAYER WITH THE YEAR SHE WON THE LADIES' SINGLES TITLE AT WIMBLEDON

11.	Serena Williams	1990
12.	Venus Williams	1976
13.	Maria Sharapova	1973
14.	Steffi Graf	2001
15.	Conchita Martinez	1977
16.	Martina Navratilova	1971
17.	Evonne Goolagong	1996
18.	Chris Evert	2002
19.	Virginia Wade	2004
20.	Billie Jean King	1994

WIMBLEDON - 1975

21. Who won the Men's Singles title?

22. Can you recall the American Runner-Up in the Men's Singles?

23. Who did the player in Q21 beat in the Semi-Finals?

24. Who did the player in Q22 beat in the Semi-Finals?

25. Name the American that won the Ladies' Singles title.

26. Name the losing Finalist, and former Champion, in the Ladies' Singles.

27. Can you name the player, and former Champion, who lost her Semi-Final match in the Ladies' Singles to the eventual Champion?

28. Name either of the USA winning pair in the Men's Doubles.

29. Can you name either of the winning pair in the Ladies' Doubles?

30. Name either of the winning pair in the Mixed Doubles.

DAVIS CUP WINNERS - 1

ALL YOU HAVE TO DO HERE IS ASSOCIATE THE COUNTRY WITH THE YEAR IT WON THE DAVIS CUP

31.	Great Britain	2002
32.	Australia	1989
33.	South Africa	1978
34.	France	1974
35.	Russia	1980
36.	Sweden	2001
37.	Czechoslovakia	1977
38.	USA	1976
39.	Germany	1975
40.	Italy	1935

PAST MASTER - JIMMY CONNORS

41. What is Jimmy's middle name - Bud, Rod or Scott?

42. How many times did Jimmy win the Men's Singles title at Wimbledon?

43. Name any year in which Jimmy won the Men's Singles title at Wimbledon.

44. How many times was Jimmy Runner-Up in the Men's Singles at Wimbledon?

45. Name any year in which Jimmy was Runner-Up in the Men's Singles at Wimbledon.

46. To the nearest 10, how many Singles titles did Jimmy win during his career?

47. In what year did Jimmy turn Professional - 1971, 1972 or 1973?

48. Who did Jimmy beat to win his first Men's Singles title at Wimbledon?

49. Can you name the last player to have beaten Jimmy in the Wimbledon Men's Singles Final?

50. How many times did Jimmy win the Men's US Open title?

LEGEND - TRACEY AUSTIN

51. In what state in the USA was Tracey born?

52. What is Tracey's middle name - Ann, Catherine or Janet?

53. What "age limit" tournament did Tracey win aged 10 in 1972?

54. Can you name the Grand Slam event in which she reached the last 8 when she was only 14?

55. In what year was Tracey ranked the No. 1 Ladies' player in the world - 1980, 1981 or 1982?

56. How many Grand Slam events did Tracey win during her career?

57. Name any Grand Slam Tournament Tracey won.

58. What European country's Singles title did Tracey win 3 times?

59. In what year did Tracey turn Professional - 1977, 1978 or 1979?

60. What Team was Tracey a winning member of in 1978, 1979 & 1980?

WIMBLEDON - 2004

61. Who won the Men's Singles title?

62. Who was Runner-Up to the player in Q61?

63. Name either of the 2 beaten Men's Singles Semi-Finalists.

64. Who won the Ladies' Singles title?

65. Who was Runner-Up to the player in Q64?

66. Name either of the 2 beaten Ladies' Singles Semi-Finalists.

67. Can you name the player who put Tim Henman out?

68. How far did Tim Henman reach in the competition?

69. In what Round was Venus Williams surprisingly knocked out?

70. What fellow American did Serena Williams defeat in the Quarter-Finals?

PAST MASTER - BJORN BORG

71. How many times did Bjorn win the Men's Singles title at Wimbledon?

72. In what year did he win his first Wimbledon Men's Singles title?

73. Who did Bjorn beat in Q72?

74. Can you name the only player to have beaten Bjorn in the Men's Singles Final at Wimbledon?

75. Name the player Bjorn beat in 2 Men's Finals at Wimbledon.

76. Apart from the players in Q74 & Q75, what other American did Bjorn beat in the Men's Singles Final at Wimbledon?

77. Bjorn never won the US Open but how many times did he reach the Final?

78. In 1974, aged 17, what Open did he win and thereby become the youngest winner of at the time?

79. Can you recall what brand of sportswear Bjorn wore during his Wimbledon glory days?

80. How many Singles titles did he win during his career - 62, 82 or 102?

WIMBLEDON - 2003

81. Who won the Men's Singles title?

82. Who was Runner-Up to the player in Q81?

83. Name either of the 2 beaten Men's Singles Semi-Finalists.

84. Who won the Ladies' Singles title?

85. Who was Runner-Up to the player in Q84?

86. Name either of the 2 beaten Ladies' Singles Semi-Finalists.

87. Was Tim Henman seeded 4th, 7th or 10th?

88. Who won a record-equalling 20th title at Wimbledon?

89. Can you recall the Men's No. 2 seed from the USA?

90. Name the Australian who won a record-equalling 8th Wimbledon Men's Doubles title.

WIMBLEDON - 1976

91. Who won the Men's Singles title?

92. Can you recall the Runner-Up in the Men's Singles?

93. What American did the player in Q91 beat in the Semi-Finals?

94. Name the "Raul" that the player in Q92 beat in the Semi-Finals.

95. Who won the Ladies Singles title?

96. Name the losing Finalist in the Ladies' Singles.

97. Can you name the player, and future Champion, who lost her Semi-Final match in the Ladies' Singles to the eventual Champion?

98. Name either of the winning pair in the Men's Doubles.

99. Can you name either of the winning pair in the Ladies' Doubles, one of them a Wimbledon Champion and the other a future Wimbledon Champion?

100. Name either of the winning pair (Australia & France) in the Mixed Doubles.

MEN'S ATP FINAL RANKINGS FOR 2004

ALL YOU HAVE TO DO HERE IS ASSOCIATE THE PLAYER WITH HIS ATP RANKING AT THE END OF THE 2004 SEASON

101.	G Gaudio	6
102.	G Coria	4
103.	R Federer	8
104.	A Agassi	3
105.	D Nalbandian	5
106.	C Moya	1
107.	T Henman	2
108.	A Roddick	10
109.	M Safin	9
110.	L Hewitt	7

LADIES' WTP FINAL RANKINGS FOR 2004

ALL YOU HAVE TO DO HERE IS ASSOCIATE THE PLAYER WITH HER WTP RANKING AT THE END OF THE 2004 SEASON

111.	E Dementieva	2
112.	A Myskina	7
113.	J Capriati	3
114.	L Davenport	9
115.	M Sharapova	10
116.	V Williams	5
117.	A Mauresmo	8
118.	J Henin-Hardenne	6
119.	S Kuznetsova	1
120.	S Williams	4

PAST MASTER - IVAN LENDL

121. How many times did Ivan win the Men's Singles title at Wimbledon?

122. How many times was Ivan Runner-Up in the Men's Singles at Wimbledon?

123. Following on from Q122, name any year in which he was Runner-Up.

124. Can you name any player to have beaten Ivan in the Men's Singles Final at Wimbledon?

125. How many times did Ivan end the year as the No. 1 ranked player in the world?

126. Can you recall any 2 years in which Ivan was the No. 1 ranked player?

127. What Open Championship did he win for the first time in 1984?

128. How many times did Ivan win the US Open?

129. Can you name any year in which Ivan won the US Open?

130. What Masters title did he win 4 times?

VENUS WILLIAMS

131. What is the name of her father and Coach?

132. In what year did Venus make her Professional debut - 1994, 1995 or 1996?

133. In 1999 Serena and Venus became the first sisters to win a Doubles Grand Slam together in the 20th Century. Which 1 of the 4 Grand Slams did they win?

134. What was the first Grand Slam Singles tournament won by Venus?

135. What in 2000 was Venus the first woman to do since 1924?

136. In what year did she win her first Professional Ladies' Singles title?

137. Can you name the European player that she beat in the Ladies' Singles Finals of the Gold Coast, Antwerp and Amelia Island Tournaments in 2002?

138. In what "iced-tea manufacturer sponsored" Championships did she beat Anna Kournikova in the Final in 1998 to claim her second Singles title?

139. Up to 2004, how many times has Venus won the Ladies' Singles title at Wimbledon?

140. What fellow American did Venus beat in the Final to win her first Wimbledon Ladies' Singles title?

THE DAVIS CUP

141. In what year was the Davis Cup first held - 1900, 1910 or 1920?

142. What Asian country refused to play in the 1974 Davis Cup Final against South Africa to protest against apartheid?

143. Name the non-European country that beat the USA 5-0 in the 1973 Davis Cup.

144. What country has won the Davis Cup the most times?

145. Can you name the European country that won the 2001 Davis Cup but lost the Final the following year?

146. Name the European country that appeared in 7 Davis Cup Finals during the 1980s.

147. In what year did Great Britain last reach the Davis Cup Final - 1978, 1988 or 1998?

148. What country lost both the 1994 & 1995 Davis Cup Finals but triumphed in 2002?

149. The 1989 Davis Cup Final was held in Stuttgart, Germany. What country beat Sweden in the Final?

150. What country lies second to the country in Q144 with 28 wins up to their 2003 victory?

WIMBLEDON - 1977

151. Who won the Men's Singles title?

152. Can you recall the Runner-Up, and former Champion, in the Men's Singles?

153. What American did the player in Q151 beat in the Semi-Finals?

154. Name the future Champion that the player in Q152 beat in the Semi-Finals.

155. Who won the Ladies' Singles title?

156. Can you name the Dutch Runner-Up in the Ladies' Singles Final?

157. Can you name the player, and former Champion, who lost her Semi-Final match in the Ladies' Singles to the eventual Champion?

158. Name either of the Australian winning pair in the Men's Doubles.

159. Can you name either of the winning pair in the Ladies' Doubles, one of them a former Wimbledon Singles Champion?

160. Name either of the South African winning pair in the Mixed Doubles.

DAVIS CUP WINNERS - 2

ALL YOU HAVE TO DO HERE IS ASSOCIATE THE COUNTRY WITH THE YEAR IT WON THE DAVIS CUP

161.	Australia	1981
162.	USA	2000
163.	Germany	1987
164.	Sweden	1993
165.	France	1983
166.	Spain	1973
167.	USA	1988
168.	Australia	1985
169.	Germany	1991
170.	Sweden	1995

LEGEND - BILLIE JEAN KING

171. What is Billie Jean's maiden name - Matthews, Meacher or Moffitt?

172. What was the first title Billie Jean won at Wimbledon?

173. How many titles did Billie Jean win at Wimbledon - 20, 21 or 22?

174. What future Wimbledon record holder partnered Billie Jean to the Ladies' Doubles crown at Wimbledon in 1979?

175. How many Wimbledon Ladies' Singles titles did Billie Jean win?

176. In what year did she win her last Wimbledon Ladies' Singles title?

177. What Team was Billie Jean the Player-Captain of in 1965 & 1976?

178. Name any 1 of the 3 players who won gold medals at the Olympic Games with Billie Jean as their Team Manager.

179. To the nearest 10, how many Professional tournaments did Billie Jean win?

180. Apart from Wimbledon, in what Championship in 1972 did Billie Jean enjoy both Singles & Doubles victories?

DAVIS CUP HOSTS IN THE 1980s

ALL YOU HAVE TO DO HERE IS MATCH THE CITY WITH THE YEAR IT HOSTED THE DAVIS CUP FINAL DURING THE 1980s

181.	Prague	1988
182.	Stuttgart	1981
183.	Gothenburg	1989
184.	Melbourne	1980
185.	Grenoble	1984
186.	Gothenburg	1985
187.	Cincinnati	1986
188.	Melbourne	1987
189.	Munich	1983
190.	Gothenburg	1982

MEN'S SINGLES CHAMPION - 2

ALL YOU HAVE TO DO HERE IS ASSOCIATE THE PLAYER WITH THE YEAR HE WON THE MEN'S SINGLES TITLE AT WIMBLEDON

191.	Stefan Edberg	1983
192.	Rod Laver	1992
193.	Boris Becker	1972
194.	John McEnroe	1998
195.	Arthur Ashe	1982
196.	Pete Sampras	1985
197.	Andre Agassi	1968
198.	Jimmy Connors	1977
199.	Bjorn Borg	1990
200.	Stan Smith	1975

LADIES' SINGLES CHAMPION - 2

ALL YOU HAVE TO DO HERE IS ASSOCIATE THE PLAYER WITH THE YEAR SHE WON THE LADIES' SINGLES TITLE AT WIMBLEDON

201.	Venus Williams	1969
202.	Jana Novotna	1989
203.	Evonne Cawley	1998
204.	Martina Hingis	1975
205.	Steffi Graf	1980
206.	Martina Navratilova	1999
207.	Ann Jones	1981
208.	Chris Evert Lloyd	2000
209.	Lindsay Davenport	1985
210.	Billie Jean King	1997

PAST MASTER - LEW HOAD

211. What nationality is Lew?

212. How many times did Lew win the Men's Singles title at Wimbledon?

213. What is his middle name - Alan, John or Wilson?

214. In what year did Lew turn Professional - 1955, 1956 or 1957?

215. What medical problem forced Lew to retire during the mid-1960s?

216. Can you name Lew's teammate when they won the Davis Cup in 1953 & 1955?

217. Lew and his Doubles partner won 3 of the 4 Grand Slam Doubles titles in 1953. Which one did they miss out on?

218. In what year was Lew ranked the No. 1 player in the world - 1955, 1956 or 1957?

219. How many Grand Slam singles titles did Lew win?

220. In what Grand Slam did Lew win a Singles title, a Doubles title and a Mixed Doubles title during his career?

WIMBLEDON - 1978

221. Who won the Men's Singles title?

222. Can you recall the Runner-Up in the Men's Singles?

223. What "Tom" did the player in Q221 beat in the Semi-Finals?

224. Name the American that the player in Q222 beat in the Semi-Finals.

225. Who won the first of her many Ladies' Singles titles?

226. Name the losing Finalist from the USA in the Ladies' Singles.

227. Can you name the British player who lost her Semi-Final match in the Ladies' Singles to the eventual Runner-Up?

228. Name either of the South African winning pair in the Men's Doubles.

229. Can you name either of the Australian winning pair in the Ladies' Doubles?

230. Name the former Dutch Runner-Up in the Ladies' Singles Final who partnered Frew McMillan to success in the Mixed Doubles.

THE NEARLY WOMEN

ALL YOU HAVE TO DO HERE IS ASSOCIATE THE PLAYER WITH THE YEAR SHE LOST THE LADIES' SINGLES FINAL AT WIMBLEDON

231.	Justine Henin-Hardenne	1999
232.	Venus Williams	1981
233.	Chris Evert Lloyd	1995
234.	Jana Novotna	1988
235.	Arantxa Sanchez-Vicario	2001
236.	Betty Stove	1984
237.	Nathalie Tauziat	1977
238.	Hana Mandlikova	1998
239.	Steffi Graf	2003
240.	Martina Navratilova	1997

PAST MASTER - JAN KODES

241. What nationality is Jan?

242. Can you recall the No. 1 Australian seed that Jan knocked out of the 1971 US Open in the 1st Round?

243. How many times did Jan win the Men's Singles title at Wimbledon?

244. Name any year in which Jan won the Men's Singles title at Wimbledon.

245. What was Jan's highest ever placing in the ATP rankings - 3rd, 4th or 5th?

246. Can you recall the maverick player that Jan beat in the Final of the 1971 French Open?

247. How many times did Jan win the French Open?

248. Can you name the American player who beat Jan in the 1971 US Open Final?

249. What Championship did he win in 1966, 1967, 1969 & 1972?

250. What Cup did he win in 1980?

LEGEND - MARIA BUENO

251. What nationality is Maria?

252. What is Maria's middle name - Catherine, Esther or Frances?

253. How many times did Maria win the Ladies' Singles title at Wimbledon?

254. In what year was she first crowned Wimbledon Champion - 1959, 1960 or 1961?

255. How many times did Maria win the Doubles title at Wimbledon?

256. Name any year in which Maria was ranked the No. 1 player in the world.

257. What Grand Slam event proved to be Maria's last?

258. What was the first Wimbledon title Maria won - Doubles, Mixed Doubles or Singles?

259. What country's Amateur Final in 1968 was the last major Final Maria appeared in?

260. How many US Open Singles titles did Maria win?

WIMBLEDON - 1979

261. Who won the Men's Singles title?

262. Can you recall the American Runner-Up in the Men's Singles?

263. What former Champion did the player in Q261 beat in the Semi-Finals?

264. Name the "Pat" that the player in Q262 beat in the Semi-Finals.

265. Who won the Ladies' Singles title?

266. Name the losing Finalist from the USA in the Ladies' Singles.

267. Can you name the Australian player who lost her Semi-Final match in the Ladies' Singles to the eventual Runner-Up?

268. Can you name either of the winning pair in the Men's Doubles, one of whom would go on to be a Wimbledon Singles Champion in his career?

269. Can you name either of the winning USA pair in the Ladies' Doubles?

270. Name either of the winning pair in the Mixed Doubles.

WIMBLEDON - 1980

271. Who won the Men's Singles title?

272. Can you recall the Runner-Up from the USA in the Men's Singles?

273. What "Brian" did the player in Q271 beat in the Semi-Finals?

274. Name the former Champion that the player in Q272 beat in the Semi-Finals.

275. Can you name the non-American who won the Ladies' Singles title?

276. Name the losing Finalist in the Ladies' Singles.

277. Can you name the USA teenager who lost her Semi-Final match in the Ladies' Singles to the eventual Winner?

278. Name either of the winning Australian pair in the Men's Doubles.

279. Can you name either of the winning USA pair in the Ladies' Doubles?

280. Name either of the winning brother & sister pair in the Mixed Doubles.

THE FRENCH OPEN

281. In what city is the French Open played each year?

282. Can you name the tennis stadium that plays host to the French Open Final?

283. In what year was the first French Open staged at the tennis stadium in Q282 - 1928, 1929 or 1930?

284. Apart from tennis, what other occupation did the man after whom the stadium in Q282 was named have?

285. In what year was the first French Open staged - 1891, 1901 or 1911?

286. Up to 2005, who was the last French player to win the Ladies' or Men's Singles title at the French Open?

287. In what year did the player in Q286 win the title?

288. Up to 2005, how many French men have won the Men's Singles title in the French Open - 2, 5 or 8?

289. What is the first Wednesday of the French Open commonly known as because the children are given the day off school to watch their favourite tennis players?

290. Up to 2005, how many French women have won the Ladies' Singles title in the French Open - 3, 6 or 9?

THE AUSTRALIAN OPEN

291. Name the month in which the Australian Open is traditionally held.

292. In what year was the tournament first held - 1903, 1904 or 1905?

293. By what name was the Australian Open originally known?

294. In what year did the tournament adopt its current name of The Australian Open - 1968, 1969 or 1970?

295. To what city did the tournament permanently move to during the 1970s?

296. Can you name the nearby country where the Australian Open was played in 1906 & 1912?

297. Can you name the Australian player who holds the record of being both the youngest and oldest winner of the Men's Singles title in the Australian Open?

298. Who in 1997, aged 16, became the youngest winner of the Ladies' Singles title in the Australian Open?

299. Who won the 2004 Men's Singles?

300. Who won the 2004 Ladies' Singles?

THE GRAND SLAM

301. Name the 4 tournaments that make up the Grand Slam.

302. Which one of the Majors is the only one that is played on clay?

303. Who in 1953 became the first female player to win the Grand Slam?

304. Can you name the Australian who is the only player, male or female, in the history of tennis to win the Grand Slam twice, i.e. all 4 Majors in the same year?

305. Name the "Donald" who in 1938 became the first player to win the Grand Slam.

306. Which Major is the second one to be played during the year on the Tennis Circuit?

307. Which one of the Majors is the oldest?

308. On what type of turf is the US Open played?

309. Can you name the player who achieved the Ladies' Grand Slam in 1988?

310. Name the famous Australian player who won the Ladies' Grand Slam in 1970.

WIMBLEDON - 1981

311. Who won the Men's Singles title?

312. Can you recall the Runner-Up in the Men's Singles?

313. What "Rod" did the player in Q311 beat in the Semi-Finals?

314. Name the former Champion that the player in Q312 beat in the Semi-Finals.

315. Who won the Ladies' Singles title?

316. The losing Finalist in the Ladies' Singles was from Czechoslovakia. Name her.

317. Can you name the former Champion who lost her Semi-Final match in the Ladies' Singles to the eventual Runner-Up?

318. Name either of the winning USA pair in the Men's Doubles.

319. Can you name either of the winning USA pair that won the first of their many Ladies' Doubles titles?

320. Name either of the winning pair, representing the Netherlands & South Africa, that won their second Mixed Doubles title.

MEN'S FRENCH OPEN CHAMPIONS - 1

ALL YOU HAVE TO DO HERE IS ASSOCIATE THE PLAYER WITH THE YEAR HE WON THE MEN'S FRENCH OPEN

321.	Jim Courier	2000
322.	Juan Carlos Ferrero	1984
323.	Ivan Lendl	2002
324.	Yevgeny Kafelnikov	2004
325.	Albert Costa	1999
326.	Michael Chang	2003
327.	Andre Agassi	1981
328.	Gaston Gaudio	1992
329.	Gustavo Kuerten	1989
330.	Bjorn Borg	1996

DAVIS CUP FINAL - 2004

331. What European country won the 2004 Davis Cup?

332. Can you recall the non-European Runners-Up?

333. Name the European country that played host to the Finals.

334. What was the Final score - 3-2, 4-1 or 5-0?

335. Can you name the player who by winning his Singles match gave his country the Davis Cup?

336. Following on from Q335, name the 2004 Grand Slam tournament Runner-Up he beat.

337. In what southern city was the Davis Cup Final played?

338. Name any 2 of the 4 players from the winning team.

339. Name any 2 of the 4 players from the Runners-Up.

340. Who was the Team Captain of the Runners-Up?

2004 WINNERS

ALL YOU HAVE TO DO HERE IS ASSOCIATE THE PLAYER WITH THE TOURNAMENT THEY WON IN 2004

341.	Roger Federer	Masters
342.	Justine Henin-Hardenne	Wimbledon
343.	Roger Federer	Masters
344.	Anastasia Myskina	US Open
345.	Roger Federer	French Open
346.	Maria Sharapova	French Open
347.	Gaston Gaudio	Wimbledon
348.	Svetlana Kuznetsova	Australian Open
349.	Roger Federer	US Open
350.	Maria Sharapova	Australian Open

LADIES' FRENCH OPEN CHAMPIONS - 1

ALL YOU HAVE TO DO HERE IS ASSOCIATE THE PLAYER WITH THE YEAR SHE WON THE LADIES' FRENCH OPEN

351.	Monica Seles	1996
352.	Arantxa Sanchez-Vicario	1969
353.	Steffi Graf	1974
354.	Chris Evert	1976
355.	Sue Barker	2000
356.	Martina Navratilova	2001
357.	Jennifer Capriati	1994
358.	Mary Pierce	1972
359.	Billie Jean King	1990
360.	Margaret Smith Court	1984

PAST MASTER - BORIS BECKER - 1

361. In what year did Boris win his first Wimbledon Men's Singles title - 1984, 1985 or 1986?

362. What age was Boris when he won the Wimbledon Men's Singles title for the first time?

363. How many times did Boris win the Wimbledon Men's Singles title?

364. Apart from the year in Q361, name any other year Boris won the Wimbledon Men's Singles title.

365. On how many occasions did Boris finish Runner-Up in the Wimbledon Men's Singles Final?

366. Following on from Q365, can you recall any year in which he was Runner-Up?

367. Who did Boris beat in his first Wimbledon Men's Singles Final?

368. Can you name the player Boris lost 2 Wimbledon Men's Singles Finals to?

369. Boris lost a Wimbledon Men's Singles Final to a fellow countryman. Name him.

370. Name the player who beat Boris in his last Wimbledon Men's Singles Final.

WORLD TEAM CUP 2004

371. Name the South American winners of the 2004 World Team Cup.

372. What Southern Hemisphere country was the losing Finalists?

373. What colour of Group did the winners top?

374. What colour of Group did the losing Finalists top?

375. Name either of the 2 players from the winning country that played a Singles match in the Final.

376. Name either of the 2 players from the Runners-Up that played a Singles match in the Final.

377. Following on from Q373, name the European country that finished Runner-Up in this Group.

378. Following on from Q374, what South American country finished Runner-Up in this Group?

379. What was the score in the Final - 2-1, 3-1 or 4-1?

380. Can you recall the name of the sponsor of the tournament - ARAG, BASF or BOSE?

DELTA TOUR OF CHAMPIONS - 2000 (Past Masters Tour)

381. Can you name the American and former multiple Wimbledon Champion who won the Final in Dublin, Ireland in February?

382. Name the French player who had to retire from the Final in Naples, Florida, USA in March.

383. Two Swedish players met in the Final in Doha, Qatar in April. Who won?

384. Can you name the Swedish player who lost his second consecutive Final when Anders Jarryd beat him in Mallorca in April?

385. Name the American multiple US Open Men's Singles winner who beat Mansour Bahrami on the opening day of the tournament held in Richmond, Virginia, USA in April.

386. Name the Swedish winner of the tournament staged in New York, USA in June when he beat Henri Leconte in the Final.

387. This Australian and former Wimbledon Champion won the tournament staged in San Diego in July. Name him.

388. Can you name the French "Guy" that won the competition held in Paris, France in September?

389. This former multiple Men's Singles Champion won 5 consecutive Finals between September and November. Can you name him?

390. Who beat John McEnroe in the last Final of the year which was held in London, England - Pat Cash, Henri Leconte or Mats Wilander?

2004 CHAMPIONS TOUR RANKINGS

ALL YOU HAVE TO DO HERE IS ASSOCIATE THE PLAYER WITH HIS RANKING

391.	Mats Wilander	Joint 16th
392.	Jim Courier	7th
393.	Pat Cash	Joint 20th
394.	John McEnroe	3rd
395.	Boris Becker	14th
396.	Felip Dewulf	1st
397.	Sergi Bruguera	15th
398.	Guy Forget	10th
399.	Jim Siemerink	6th
400.	Mikael Pernfors	5th

MEN'S US OPEN CHAMPIONS - 2

ALL YOU HAVE TO DO HERE IS ASSOCIATE THE PLAYER WITH THE YEAR HE WON THE MEN'S US OPEN

401.	Patrick Rafter	1977
402.	Pete Sampras	1989
403.	Andre Agassi	1991
404.	Mats Wilander	1980
405.	Boris Becker	1987
406.	Guillermo Vilas	1983
407.	Jimmy Connors	1988
408.	Stefan Edberg	1999
409.	John McEnroe	1998
410.	Ivan Lendl	1996

LADIES' US OPEN CHAMPIONS - 2

ALL YOU HAVE TO DO HERE IS ASSOCIATE THE PLAYER WITH THE YEAR SHE WON THE LADIES' US OPEN

411.	Billie Jean King	1999
412.	Venus Williams	1973
413.	Lindsay Davenport	1975
414.	Margaret Smith Court	1998
415.	Arantxa Sanchez-Vicario	1983
416.	Serena Williams	1974
417.	Steffi Graf	1991
418.	Chris Evert	1994
419.	Monica Seles	1996
420.	Martina Navratilova	2001

THE 2000 OLYMPIC GAMES

421. What Russian player won the Men's Singles gold medal?

422. Can you name the German player who won the silver medal in the Men's Singles Final?

423. Name the USA player who won the Ladies' Singles gold medal.

424. Can you recall the Russian silver medal winner in the Ladies' Singles?

425. Can you recall the name of either of the 2 "home" players who lost the Men's Doubles Final to Canada's Sebastien Lareau and Daniel Nestor?

426. Can you recall the name of the future Wimbledon Men's Singles Champion who lost the bronze medal match to France's Arnaud Di Pasquale?

427. Name the American bronze medal winner in the Ladies' Singles.

428. Can you name the Australian player that the player in Q427 beat to win the bronze medal?

429. How many players took part in both the Men's and Ladies' Singles - 32, 64 or 128?

430. What country staged the Olympic Games?

MEN'S FRENCH OPEN CHAMPIONS - 2

ALL YOU HAVE TO DO HERE IS ASSOCIATE THE PLAYER WITH THE YEAR HE WON THE MEN'S FRENCH OPEN

431.	Jim Courier	1976
432.	Carlos Moya	1993
433.	Ivan Lendl	1990
434.	Thomas Muster	1991
435.	Mats Wilander	1971
436.	Sergi Bruguera	1987
437.	Andres Gomez	2001
438.	Jan Kodes	1988
439.	Gustavo Kuerten	1998
440.	Bjorn Borg	1995

LADIES' FRENCH OPEN CHAMPIONS - 2

ALL YOU HAVE TO DO HERE IS ASSOCIATE THE PLAYER WITH THE YEAR SHE WON THE LADIES' FRENCH OPEN

441.	Mima Jausovec	1992
442.	Chris Evert Lloyd	1997
443.	Serena Williams	1982
444.	Hana Mandlikova	1999
445.	Martina Navratilova	1989
446.	Arantxa Sanchez-Vicario	1977
447.	Steffi Graf	1981
448.	Monica Seles	1975
449.	Iva Majoli	1980
450.	Chris Evert	2002

PAST MASTER - BORIS BECKER - 2

451. In how many Wimbledon Men's Singles Finals did Boris appear between 1985 - 1995?

452. When Boris won the Men's Singles title at Wimbledon in 1985 he was the youngest ever winner of a Grand Slam tournament (17 years & 7 months). Who in 1989 took this record from him by winning the French Open?

453. Name any year in which Boris was the Runner-Up in the ATP Tour World Championships.

454. What major tennis tournament did Boris win in 1988?

455. In what year did he win his only US Open title?

456. How many times did he win the Australian Open?

457. Following on from Q456, name any year he won the Australian Open.

458. At what Olympic Games did Boris win a gold medal in the Doubles competition?

459. What Team did he manage in 1997?

460. What was the highest ever ranking Boris achieved in Men's Doubles - 2nd, 4th or 6th?

WORLD TEAM CUP - 2003

461. What South American country won the 2003 World Team Cup?

462. This Eastern European country was the losing Finalist. Name it.

463. What colour of Group did the winners top?

464. What colour of Group did the losing Finalists top?

465. Name either of the 2 players from the winning country that played a Singles match in the Final.

466. Name either of the 2 players from the Runners-Up that played a Singles match in the Final.

467. Following on from Q463, what South American country finished Runner-Up in this Group?

468. Following on from Q464, what country finished Runner-Up in this Group?

469. What was the score in the Final?

470. Can you recall the country that played host to the tournament?

SERENA WILLIAMS

471. Including the 2004 Championship, how many times has Serena won the Ladies' Singles title at Wimbledon?

472. What fellow American did Serena beat in the Final to win her first Wimbledon Ladies' Singles title?

473. Serena played in her first Grand Slam Singles event in 1998 and went out losing to her sister. In which 1 of the 4 Grand Slams events did she participate?

474. In what year did she win her first WTA Singles title?

475. Following on from Q474, can you name the French player she beat in the Final?

476. What was the first Grand Slam Singles tournament won by Serena?

477. Can you name the American player that beat her in the Quarter-Finals of both the French Open & Wimbledon in 2001?

478. Can you recall the second Grand Slam Singles title she won?

479. In 2002 Serena met the same European player in the Final of successive tournaments in Germany and Italy. Who did she lose to in Berlin but beat in Rome?

480. What age was Serena when she turned Professional?

WTA SANEX CHAMPIONSHIPS - 2001

481. Which one of the Williams sisters won the tournament?

482. Can you name the American player who finished as the Runner-Up?

483. Name either of the 2 beaten Semi-Finalists.

484. The American No. 1 seed for the tournament was beaten in the 2nd Round. Name her.

485. Can you name the "Jelena" who was seeded 6th for the tournament?

486. In what German city was the tournament held?

487. How much, to the nearest $100,000, did the winner receive?

488. Can you name the 3-times winner of the French Open who was beaten by Kim Clijsters in the 2nd Round?

489. Apart from Kim Clijsters, can you name the other Belgian player who made it into the 2nd Round?

490. What seeding was the eventual winner of the Championships given at the start of the tournament - 2nd, 4th or 7th?

WTA HOME DEPOT CHAMPIONSHIPS - 2002

491. Can you name the Belgian player who won the tournament?

492. Can you name the American player who finished as the Runner-Up?

493. Name either of the 2 beaten American Semi-Finalists.

494. What German car manufacturer "presented" the tournament?

495. The European No. 4 seed for the tournament was beaten in the 2nd Round. Name her.

496. Can you name the Slovakian player who was seeded 7th for the tournament?

497. In what Californian city was the tournament held?

498. How much, to the nearest $125,000, did the winner receive?

499. Can you name the Russian player who lost in the 1st Round?

500. A former American Wimbledon Ladies' Singles Champion lost to Monica Seles in the 1st Round. Name her.

THE BOYS' SINGLES FINAL AT WIMBLEDON

501. Who was the last player to win the Boys' Singles Championship at Wimbledon and then go on to win the Men's Singles?

502. What nationality was the winner of the first Boys' Singles Championship at Wimbledon in 1947 - American, British or Danish?

503. Can you name the Runner-Up in the 1994 Boys' Singles Championship at Wimbledon, who went on to lose the Men's Singles Championship 9 years later?

504. Can you name the future Australian-born Wimbledon Men's Singles Champion who lost the Boys' Singles Championship at Wimbledon in 1981 but came back the following year to win the Boys' title?

505. Name the Swedish player who won the 1983 Boys' Singles Championship at Wimbledon and then went on to win the Men's title twice in his career.

506. Can you name the winner of the 1972 Boys' Singles Championship at Wimbledon who went on to greater success in the Men's Singles during his career?

507. Name the New Zealand-born winner of the Boys' Singles Championship at Wimbledon in 1975 who lost the 1983 Men's Singles Final to John McEnroe.

508. He lost the Men's Singles Final at Wimbledon in 1986 & 1987 but won the Boys' Singles Championship in 1978. Name him.

509. How many times did Boris Becker win the Boys' Singles Championship at Wimbledon?

510. Who was the last Wimbledon Men's Singles Finalist to appear in the Final of the Boys' Singles Championship at Wimbledon?

WIMBLEDON BOYS' SINGLES CHAMPIONS

511.	F Mergea (ROM)	2001
512.	N Mahut (FRA)	1995
513.	W Whitehouse (RSA)	2002
514.	J Melzer (AUT)	2004
515.	V Voltchkov (BLR)	2003
516.	S Humphries (USA)	2000
517.	T Reid (AUS)	1996
518.	G Monfils (FRA)	1997
519.	R Valent (SUI)	1994
520.	O Mutis (FRA)	1999

PAST MASTER - ARTHUR ASHE

521. What is Arthur's middle name - James, Robert or William?

522. Can you recall the highest rank Arthur reached in the US Army?

523. What was the first Grand Slam tournament that Arthur won?

524. In what year did Arthur win the Men's Singles title at Wimbledon - 1973, 1974 or 1975?

525. Name the fellow countryman Arthur beat in the Wimbledon Men's Singles Final.

526. Apart from the Grand Slams in Q523 & Q524, what was the other Grand Slam tournament he won?

527. When the USA won the Davis Cup in 1968, how many Singles matches did he win in succession - 7, 9 or 11?

528. How many Davis Cup tournaments did he take part in to place him in 3rd place on the USA list of most Davis Cup competitions?

529. When Arthur won the Men's Singles title at Wimbledon was he seeded 1st, 3rd or 6th?

530. Name either of the 2 Grand Slam Mens' Doubles he won.

PAST MASTER - JAROSLAV DROBNY

531. In what country was Jaroslav born?

532. What nationality did he adopt from 1949-1954 - American, Australian or Egyptian?

533. Was Jaroslav a left or right handed player?

534. In what year did Jaroslav gain British citizenship - 1954, 1955 or 1956?

535. What sport did Jaroslav play competitively in the winter months?

536. How many Men's Wimbledon Singles titles did he win?

537. What Grand Slam tournament did he win in 1951 and retain in 1952?

538. What was the only Grand Slam tournament in which Jaroslav won the Men's Doubles title?

539. In what year's Olympics did he win a silver medal - 1948, 1952 or 1956?

540. Can you name the 19-year-old Australian player, and former Australian & French Men's Singles Champion, that Jaroslav beat in the Final of the Men's Singles at Wimbledon?

WIMBLEDON RECORDS

541. What country has produced the most Men's Singles Champions?

542. What country has produced the most Ladies' Singles Champions?

543. Name the USA player who holds the joint-record for the most Men's Singles titles.

544. Can you name the British player who holds the joint-record with the player in Q543?

545. Who has won the most Ladies' Doubles Championships?

546. What is the most Mixed Doubles Championships any male player has won?

547. What is the most Mixed Doubles Championships any female player has won?

548. Up to and including 2004, what country lies 3rd in the overall table for providing the most Men's Singles Champions with 21 in total?

549. Who is the youngest ever Men's Singles Champion?

550. Can you name the Australian player who holds the record for being the youngest ever Mixed Doubles Champion?

LADIES' DOUBLES WINNERS AT WIMBLEDON

ALL YOU HAVE TO DO HERE IS ASSOCIATE THE WINNING PARTNERSHIP WITH THE YEAR THEY WON THE LADIES' DOUBLES AT WIMBLEDON

551.	Mrs L W King & Miss M Navratilova	1998
552.	Miss M Navratilova & Miss P Shriver	2002
553.	Miss K Clijsters & Miss A Sugiyama	1983
554.	Miss M Hingis & Miss J Novotna	1989
555.	Miss B C Fernandez & Miss N M Zvereva	1976
556.	Miss V E Williams & Miss S J Williams	1977
557.	Miss K Jordan & Miss P D Smylie	1993
558.	Miss J Novotna & Miss H Sukova	1985
559.	Mrs R L Cawley & Miss J C Russell	1979
560.	Miss C M Evert & Miss M Navratilova	2003

VIRGINIA SLIMS CHAMPIONSHIP WINNERS

ALL YOU HAVE TO DO HERE IS ASSOCIATE THE PLAYER WITH THE YEAR SHE WON THE CHAMPIONSHIP

561.	Chris Evert	1977
562.	Martina Navratilova	1974
563.	Rosie Casals	1973
564.	Evonne Goolagong	1983
565.	Virginia Wade	1984
566.	Wendy Turnbull	1985
567.	Martina Navratilova	1976
568.	Martina Navratilova	1975
569.	Chris Evert	1978
570.	Martina Navratilova	1972

LADIES' DOUBLES AT WIMBLEDON

(Up to and including 2004)

571. How many titles have the Williams sisters won?

572. When was the last year it was an all "Miss" Final?

573. Can you recall the last year in which a "Mrs" won the title?

574. Who partnered Steffi Graf to victory in 1988?

575. Name either of the 2 winners from 2004.

576. Can you recall the name of either of the 2 Russian winners in 1991?

577. Name the Czechoslovakian player who partnered Martina Hingis to victory in 1996.

578. This USA player lost the 1998 Final with Miss N M Zvereva but came back the next year and won with Miss C M Morariu. Name her.

579. Name the Spanish player who partnered Jana Novotna to victory in 1995.

580. The 1987 Final was the first time since 1978 that a USA player failed to win. Name either of the 2 European winners.

2001 SANEX LADIES' DOUBLES CHAMPIONSHIPS

581. Name either of the winning pair.

582. What 2 countries did the winning pair represent?

583. Can you recall the name of either beaten Finalist?

584. Apart from the countries in Q582 & Russia, what other country, in Africa, was represented in the Final?

585. In what city in Germany was the tournament held?

586. To the nearest $50,000, how much did the winning pair receive?

587. To the nearest $250,000, what was the total prize money on offer?

588. Name either of the 2 players the Champions beat in their Semi-Final match.

589. Apart from the players in Q588, can you name another beaten Semi-Finalist?

590. What type of turf was used for the competition?

MEN'S MULTIPLE CHAMPION

ALL YOU HAVE TO DO HERE IS ASSOCIATE THE PLAYER WITH THE NUMBER OF TIMES HE WON THE MEN'S SINGLES TITLE AT WIMBLEDON

591.	Don Budge	4
592.	John Newcombe	2
593.	Bjorn Borg	3
594.	Rod Laver	3
595.	Pete Sampras	3
596.	John McEnroe	5
597.	Jimmy Connors	7
598.	Fred Perry	5
599.	Boris Becker	2
600.	Laurie Doherty	3

MEN'S DOUBLES CHAMPIONS

ALL YOU HAVE TO DO HERE IS ASSOCIATE THE PLAYERS WITH THE YEAR THEY WON THE MEN'S DOUBLES TITLE AT WIMBLEDON

601.	2002	J Eltingh & P Haarhuis (NED)
602.	1986	P Fleming & J McEnroe (USA)
603.	2001	J Newcombe & A Roche (AUS)
604.	1998	T Woodbridge & M Woodforde (AUS)
605.	1999	J McEnroe (USA) & M Stich (GER)
606.	1978	J Nystrom & M Wilander (SWE)
607.	1996	R Hewitt & F McMillan (SA)
608.	1983	T Woodbridge (AUS) & J Bjorkman (SWE)
609.	1992	M Bhupathi & L Paes (IND)
610.	1974	D Johnson & J Palmer (USA)

LADIES' MULTIPLE CHAMPION

ALL YOU HAVE TO DO HERE IS ASSOCIATE THE PLAYER WITH THE NUMBER OF TIMES SHE WON THE LADIES' SINGLES TITLE AT WIMBLEDON

611.	Evonne Goolagong Cawley	4
612.	Louise Brough	3
613.	Martina Navratilova	6
614.	Steffi Graf	3
615.	Margaret Smith Court	6
616.	Billie Jean King	2
617.	Helen Willis Moody	7
618.	Chris Evert Lloyd	8
619.	Maureen Connolly	9
620.	Suzanne Lenglen	3

LEGEND - EVONNE GOOLAGONG CAWLEY

621. What nationality is Evonne?

622. What is her middle name - Farrah, Fay or Fiona?

623. How many times did Evonne win the Wimbledon Ladies' Singles title?

624. Following on from Q623, can you name any year in which she was crowned Champion?

625. How many times was Evonne the Runner-Up in the Wimbledon Ladies' Singles Final?

626. Name any year in which she finished Runner-Up in the Wimbledon Ladies' Singles Final.

627. Can you name any player Evonne beat in the Wimbledon Ladies' Singles Final?

628. Can you name the player Evonne lost twice to in the Wimbledon Ladies' Singles Final?

629. How many times did Evonne win the Singles title at the Australian Open?

630. Following on from Q629, can you name any year in which she was crowned Champion?

THE NEARLY MEN

ALL YOU HAVE TO DO HERE IS ASSOCIATE THE PLAYER WITH THE YEAR HE LOST THE MEN'S SINGLES FINAL AT WIMBLEDON

631.	Patrick Rafter	1987
632.	Boris Becker	1989
633.	David Nalbandian	1995
634.	Ivan Lendl	1993
635.	Goran Ivanisevic	1997
636.	Jimmy Connors	1998
637.	Stefan Edberg	2001
638.	Kevin Curren	2002
639.	Jim Courier	1975
640.	Cedric Pioline	1985

MEN'S US OPEN CHAMPIONS - 1

ALL YOU HAVE TO DO HERE IS ASSOCIATE THE PLAYER WITH THE YEAR HE WON THE MEN'S US OPEN

641.	Patrick Rafter	2000
642.	Pete Sampras	1978
643.	Andre Agassi	1986
644.	Ilie Nastase	1984
645.	Marat Safin	1968
646.	Arthur Ashe	1994
647.	Jimmy Connors	2002
648.	Lleyton Hewitt	1997
649.	John McEnroe	2001
650.	Ivan Lendl	1972

LADIES' US OPEN CHAMPIONS - 1

ALL YOU HAVE TO DO HERE IS ASSOCIATE THE PLAYER WITH THE YEAR SHE WON THE LADIES' US OPEN

651.	Martina Hingis	1992
652.	Venus Williams	1979
653.	Tracey Austin	1990
654.	Hana Mandlikova	1993
655.	Gabriela Sabatini	1987
656.	Serena Williams	1997
657.	Steffi Graf	1977
658.	Chris Evert	2000
659.	Monica Seles	1985
660.	Martina Navratilova	2002

THE 2004 OLYMPIC GAMES

661. Who won the Men's Singles gold medal?

662. Can you name the player who finished Runner-Up in the Men's Singles Final?

663. Name the European player who won the Ladies' Singles gold medal.

664. What French player was Runner-Up to the player in Q663?

665. Can you recall the name of the American No. 2 seeded player that Fernando Gonzalez beat in Round 3 of the Men's Singles?

666. What nationality is Tomas Berdych who put Roger Federer out of the Men's Singles?

667. Name either of the 2 beaten Semi-Finalists in the Men's Singles competition.

668. Name either of the 2 beaten Semi-Finalists in the Ladies' Singles competition.

669. In the Ladies' Doubles, Japan's Shinobu Asagoe and Ai Sugiyama beat the American pair in the Quarter-Finals. Name the legendary player, and multiple Champion, who partnered Lisa Raymond in the USA Team.

670. Can you name the player who won 2 gold medals?

WIMBLEDON - 1982

671. Who won his second and last Men's Singles title?

672. Can you recall the player that finished Runner-Up for the second time in his career in the Men's Singles?

673. What "Mark" did the player in Q671 beat in the Semi-Finals?

674. What "Tim" did the player in Q672 beat in the Semi-Finals?

675. Who won her third Ladies' Singles title?

676. Name the player who lost her fifth Ladies' Singles Final.

677. Can you name the former Multiple Champion who lost her Semi-Final match in the Ladies Singles to the eventual Runner-Up?

678. Name either of the Australian winning pair in the Men's Doubles who claimed their second title.

679. Can you name either of the winning pair in the Ladies' Doubles who won their second title together?

680. Name the future South African Men's Singles Runner-Up who won the Mixed Doubles title with Miss A E Smith.

PAST MASTER - STEFAN EDBERG

681. How many Grand Slam titles did Stefan win - 5, 6 or 7?

682. How many times did Stefan win the Wimbledon Men's Singles title?

683. Name any player he beat in a Wimbledon Men's Singles Final.

684. Which 1 of the 4 Grand Slams was the only Singles title Stefan failed to win?

685. When Stefan became the No. 1 ranked player in the world in August 1990, who did he replace in top spot?

686. For how many consecutive years was Stefan ranked in the world's Top 10 players?

687. What award did he win in 1991 & 1992?

688. In what Olympic Games did Stefan win the tennis gold medal?

689. How many times did Stefan win the Davis Cup with Sweden?

690. To the nearest 5, how many career Singles titles did Stefan win?

WIMBLEDON - 1983

691. Who won his second Men's Singles title?

692. Can you recall the New Zealand player who was Runner-Up in the Men's Singles?

693. Name the Czechoslovakian-born player that the player in Q691 beat in the Semi-Finals.

694. Can you name the South African player that the player in Q692 beat in the Semi-Finals?

695. Who won her fourth Ladies' Singles title?

696. Name the losing USA teenager in the Ladies' Singles Final.

697. Can you name the former Multiple Champion who lost her Semi-Final match in the Ladies Singles to the eventual Runner-Up?

698. Name the USA winning pair in the Men's Doubles who claimed their third title.

699. Can you name the USA winning pair in the Ladies' Doubles who claimed their third title?

700. Name the British player who partnered Wendy Turnbull to victory in the Mixed Doubles.

LEGEND - VIRGINIA WADE

701. In what year did Virginia win the Wimbledon Ladies' Singles title?

702. Can you recall the player she beat in the Final of Q701?

703. What was her nickname on the Professional Tennis Circuit?

704. Who presented Virginia with the Wimbledon Ladies' Singles trophy?

705. What age was Virginia when she won the Wimbledon Ladies' Singles title?

706. How many Singles Grand Slam Finals did Virginia win?

707. Can you name the only Singles Grand Slam Final she failed to win?

708. What inaugural Professional tournament did she win in 1968?

709. Following on from Q708, what "home" player did she beat in the Final?

710. To the nearest 10, how many career Singles titles did she win?

WIMBLEDON - 1984

711. Who won the Men's Singles title?

712. Can you recall the Runner-Up who appeared in his sixth and last Men's Singles Final?

713. What future Australian Men's Singles Champion did the player in Q711 beat in the Semi-Finals?

714. What future 2-times Runner-Up in the Men's Singles Final did the player in Q712 beat in the Semi-Finals?

715. Name the winner of the Ladies' Singles title.

716. Name the losing Finalist in the Ladies' Singles.

717. Can you name the former Wimbledon Ladies' Singles Champion who lost her Semi-Final match in the Ladies' Singles to the eventual Runner-Up?

718. Name either of the winning pair in the Men's Doubles.

719. Can you name either of the winning pair in the Ladies' Doubles?

720. Name the British or Australian member of the winning pair in the Mixed Doubles Final.

PAST MASTER - TONY ROCHE

721. What nationality is Tony?

722. What was the only Singles Grand Slam that Tony won?

723. What was the highest ever ranking achieved by Tony in the Men's Singles world rankings?

724. In what year did he achieve the position in Q723?

725. How many times did Tony win the Men's Doubles title at Wimbledon - 4, 5 or 6?

726. What fellow countryman partnered Tony to victory in the Finals in Q725?

727. How many Men's Doubles Grand Slam titles did Tony win with the player in Q726- 14, 15 or 16?

728. How many Singles titles did Tony win during his career - 12, 16 or 20?

729. For what Team was Tony recalled at the age of 31 in 1977?

730. Apart from the title in Q722, what other country's Singles title did Tony win in 1966?

WIMBLEDON - 1985

731. Who won the Men's Singles title?

732. Can you recall the South African player who was the Runner-Up in the Men's Singles Final?

733. What former Multiple Men's Singles Champion did the player in Q732 beat in the Semi-Finals?

734. Name the Swiss player that the player in Q731 beat in the Semi-Finals.

735. Can you name the Ladies' Singles winner?

736. Name the former Multiple Champion who appeared in her last Wimbledon Ladies' Singles Final.

737. Can you name the future American Runner-Up in a Wimbledon Ladies' Singles Final who lost her Semi-Final match in the Ladies' Singles to the eventual Champion?

738. Name either of the winning pair in the Men's Doubles representing Hungary & Switzerland.

739. Can you name either 1 of the winning pair in the Ladies' Doubles representing Australia & the USA?

740. Name the former Men's Doubles Champion or former Ladies' Doubles Champion that formed the winning pair in the Mixed Doubles Final.

LEGEND - STEFFI GRAF

741. To the nearest 10, how many career WTA Singles title did Steffi win?

742. How many Grand Slam Singles titles did Steffi win - 20, 21 or 22?

743. What Singles Grand Slam did she win the most times?

744. Can you name the first Grand Slam Singles title won by Steffi?

745. How many Grand Slam Singles Finals did Steffi lose in her career?

746. In what year did Steffi win the Grand Slam, capturing all 4 of the Major Ladies' Singles titles?

747. Can you recall the year in which Steffi was first ranked in the world's Top 10 players?

748. What Cup did she win with Germany in 1987 & 1992?

749. What age was Steffi when she retired?

750. Who did Steffi beat to win her first Wimbledon Ladies' Singles title?

WIMBLEDON - 1986

751. Who won the Men's Singles title?

752. Can you recall the Czechoslovakian-born player who was the Runner-Up in the Men's Singles Final?

753. Can you name the French player that the Champion beat in the Semi-Finals?

754. Name the fellow countryman that the Runner-Up beat in the Semi-Finals.

755. Who won the Ladies' Singles title?

756. Name the Czechoslovakian player who was Runner-Up in the Ladies' Singles Final.

757. Can you name the future Argentinean Runner-Up in a Wimbledon Ladies' Singles Final who lost her Semi-Final match in the Ladies' Singles to the eventual Champion?

758. Name either of the winning Swedish pair in the Men's Doubles Final.

759. Can you name either of the winning pair in the Ladies' Doubles representing the USA?

760. Name either USA member of the winning pair in the Mixed Doubles Final.

PAST MASTER - JOHN McENROE

761. In what year did John reach his first Wimbledon Men's Singles Final?

762. Who beat him in the game in Q761?

763. Can you name the player that John beat to win his first Wimbledon Men's Singles title?

764. How many Grand Slam Singles titles did John win?

765. What was the first Grand Slam Singles title he won?

766. In what year did John play in his last Wimbledon Men's Singles Final?

767. How many Men's Singles titles did he win at Wimbledon?

768. Name the fellow countryman that John beat to win his last Wimbledon Men's Singles Final.

769. In what year did John turn Professional - 1977, 1978 or 1979?

770. In what country in Europe was John born?

WIMBLEDON - 1987

771. Name the Australian winner of the Men's Singles title.

772. Can you recall the Runner-Up, for the second time in his career, in the Men's Singles Final?

773. Can you name the former Multiple Champion that the 1987 Champion beat in the Semi-Finals?

774. Name the future Wimbledon Men's Singles Champion that the Runner-Up in the Men's Singles Final beat in the Semi-Finals.

775. Name the winner of the Ladies' Singles title.

776. Name the future Multiple Champion who appeared in her first Wimbledon Ladies' Singles Final.

777. Can you name the former Multiple Champion who lost her Semi-Final match in the Ladies' Singles to the eventual Champion?

778. Name either of the winning USA pair in the Men's Doubles Final.

779. Can you name either of the winning non-USA pair in the Ladies' Doubles Final?

780. Name either member of the winning British pair in the Mixed Doubles Final.

LEGEND - CHRIS EVERT

781. Name the Ladies' Grand Slam winner and No. 1 ranked player in the world that a 15-year-old Chris beat in a tournament in North Carolina in 1970.

782. Chris lost to the eventual Champion in the 1970 US Open Ladies' Singles Semi-Finals. Who beat her?

783. To the nearest 25, how many Professional Singles titles did Chris win during her career?

784. In what year did she turn Professional - 1971, 1972 or 1973?

785. What was the first Grand Slam Singles title won by Chris?

786. How many times did Chris win the Wimbledon Ladies' Singles title?

787. Name any year in which Chris won the Wimbledon Ladies' Singles title.

788. Who did Chris marry in 1980?

789. Name the Russian player that Chris beat to win her first Wimbledon Ladies Singles title.

790. Can you name the Australian that beat Chris in the 1980 Wimbledon Ladies' Singles Final?

WIMBLEDON - 1988

791. Name the Swedish winner of the Men's Singles title.

792. Can you recall the former Champion that the 1988 Champion beat in the Men's Singles Final?

793. Can you name the former 2-times Finalist that the Runner-Up beat in the Semi-Finals?

794. Name the No. 1 ranked player in the world that the 1988 Champion beat in the Men's Singles Semi-Finals.

795. Can you name the future Multiple Champion who won her first Wimbledon Ladies' Singles title?

796. Name the former Multiple Champion who was the Runner-Up in the Wimbledon Ladies' Singles Final.

797. What was the name of the former Multiple Champion who lost her Semi-Final match in the Ladies' Singles to the eventual Runner-Up?

798. Do you recall the name either of the winning USA pair in the Men's Doubles Final who claimed their second Men's Doubles title?

799. Can you name either of the winning non-USA pair in the Ladies' Doubles Final?

800. Name either member of the winning USA pair in the Mixed Doubles Final.

FACTS & TRIVIA - 1

801. In what year during the 1970's did computer rankings for the world's top tennis players begin?

802. Name the player who holds her country's Federation Cup record of 28 wins and 4 losses (20-2 in Singles and 8-2 in Doubles).

803. Who is the only black male tennis player to have won 3 Grand Slam Singles titles?

804. Who in 1972 was the last British player to reach the Boys' Singles Final at Wimbledon?

805. Who in 1983 set the record as being the oldest female seed in the Ladies' Singles at Wimbledon?

806. Name the player who had a career record of 31 wins and 20 losses against Jimmy Connors, 15 wins and 21 losses against Ivan Lendl and was even with Borg (7-7).

807. Name the Swedish player who in 1987 was the last man to win the Australian Open played on grass.

808. What male player had a 66-match winning run indoors between October 1981 and January 1983?

809. He won the US Open Men's Singles in 1926 & 1927 and went on to design his own tennis clothes with his familiar crocodile trademark on them. Name him.

810. What Grand Slam Major did the The Kooyong Lawn Tennis Club play host to from 1972-1987?

WIMBLEDON - 1989

811. Who won his third and last Men's Singles title?

812. Can you recall the former Champion that the 1989 Champion beat in the Men's Singles Final?

813. Can you name the former 5-times Finalist that the Runner-up beat in the Semi-Finals?

814. Name the Czech-born player that the 1989 Champion beat in the Men's Singles Semi-Finals.

815. Name the winner of the Ladies' Singles title.

816. Name the former Multiple Champion who lost her second Wimbledon Ladies' Singles Final.

817. Can you name the former Multiple Champion who lost her Semi-Final match in the Ladies Singles to the eventual Champion?

818. Name either of the winning pair in the Men's Doubles Final who won the first of their 2 Wimbledon Men's Doubles titles.

819. Can you name either of the winning Czechoslovakian pair in the Ladies' Doubles Final?

820. Name either member of the winning pair in the Mixed Doubles Final, one of whom also won another 1989 Final at Wimbledon.

CHAMPIONS - 1

821. Name the Australian player who won the Ladies' Singles at the 1971 French Open.

822. What Championship did Jimmy Connors win at Wimbledon in 1973?

823. Name the Australian who beat Jan Kodes in the 1973 US Open Final.

824. Can you recall the fellow American that Jimmy Connors beat in a 5-set Final in the 1973 US Pro Singles?

825. Can you name the "Ellen", who had the same surname as a future President of the USA, who won the US Open Ladies' Singles in 1890?

826. In what year did Virginia Wade win the Australian Open Ladies' Singles title - 1970, 1971 or 1972?

827. Name the player who held the record for the most Ladies' Singles titles victories before Martina Navratilova bettered her record in 1992.

828. Name the player who in 1979 set an open-era record with 27 overall tournament victories (10 Singles titles & 17 Doubles titles).

829. Can you name the French winner of the French Open Men's Singles title in 1983?

830. In 1970 Margaret Smith won the Grand Slam. Name any opponent she beat in 1 of the 4 Finals.

WIMBLEDON - 1990

831. Who won the Men's Singles title?

832. Can you recall the former Champion who was Runner-Up in the Men's Singles?

833. Who did the 1990 Champion beat in the Men's Singles Semi-Finals?

834. What future Wimbledon Men's Singles Champion, and crowd favourite, did the eventual Runner-Up beat in the Men's Singles Semi-Finals?

835. Who won the Ladies' Singles title?

836. What "Zina" was the losing Finalist from the USA in the Ladies' Singles?

837. Can you name the former Champion who lost her Semi-Final match in the Ladies' Singles to the eventual Runner-Up?

838. Name either of the winning USA pair, and No. 1 seeds, in the Men's Doubles.

839. Can you name either of the winning pair from Czechoslovakia in the Ladies' Doubles?

840. Name either of the winning USA pair in the Mixed Doubles, both of whom were appearing in their second Wimbledon Final of 1990.

PAST MASTER - ILIE NASTASE

841. In what Romanian city was Ilie born?

842. How many times did Ilie win the Masters Tournament?

843. Following on from Q842, name any year in which he won the Masters.

844. How many times did Ilie win the Wimbledon Men's Singles title?

845. Name the American who was the first player to beat Ilie in the Wimbledon Men's Singles Final.

846. Who beat Ilie in the 1976 Wimbledon Men's Singles Final?

847. To the nearest 10, how many career Singles titles did he win?

848. How many times did Ilie win the Men's Singles at the US Open?

849. Following on from Q848, name any year he was Champion.

850. Of what Team was he made Captain in 1995?

WIMBLEDON - 1991

851. Name the German player who won the Men's Singles title.

852. Can you recall the Runner-Up, also from Germany, in the Men's Singles?

853. What former Champion did the eventual 1991 Champion beat in the Men's Singles Semi-Finals?

854. What "David" did the eventual Runner-Up beat in the Men's Singles Semi-Finals?

855. Who won her third Wimbledon Ladies' Singles title?

856. Name the South American losing Finalist in the Ladies' Singles.

857. Can you name either of the beaten Semi-Finalists, both from the USA, in the Ladies' Singles?

858. Name either of the winning pair in the Men's Doubles who claimed their second Wimbledon Men's Doubles title.

859. Can you name either of the winning Russian pair in the Ladies' Doubles?

860. Name either of the Australian Runners-Up in the 1990 Wimbledon Mixed Doubles Final who won the 1991 Mixed Doubles title.

WIMBLEDON - 1992

861. Name the American "heart-throb" who won the Men's Singles title.

862. Can you recall the Runner-Up from Croatia in the Men's Singles?

863. What former American Multiple Champion did the 1992 Champion beat in the Men's Singles Semi-Finals?

864. The 1992 Runner-Up beat a future Multiple Champion in the Men's Singles Semi-Finals. Can you name him?

865. Who won her fourth Ladies' Singles title?

866. Name the losing Finalist in the Ladies' Singles.

867. Can you name the former Multiple Champion who lost her Semi-Final match in the Ladies' Singles to the eventual Runner-Up?

868. Name either of the winning unseeded pair in the Men's Doubles who were both former winners of the Men's Singles at Wimbledon.

869. Can you name either of the winning pair, representing the CIS and the USA, in the Ladies' Doubles?

870. Name either of the winning pair, representing Czechoslovakia and Latvia, in the Mixed Doubles.

FACTS & TRIVIA - 2

871. Can you recall the nickname Evonne Goolagong was given by the British Press when she first appeared on the Tennis Circuit?

872. Name the female player that ended her career with a .8996 winning average, the highest in the Professional history of tennis.

873. How many weeks in total did Jimmy Connors spend as the No. 1 ranked player in the world - 248, 258 or 268?

874. In what city was Jan Kodes born?

875. Who won 13 of the 15 Men's Singles tournaments he entered in 1984?

876. Name the Swedish player who won the bronze medal in both the Men's Singles and Men's Doubles at the Olympic Games in Seoul in 1988.

877. In 1962 Rod Laver won the Grand Slam. Name any opponent he beat in 1 of the 4 Finals.

878. Who in 1973 set the record as being the youngest male seed in the Men's Singles at Wimbledon?

879. Who played for his country in the 1980 Davis Cup and had a record of 7-0 in Singles matches and 3-0 in Doubles matches?

880. Who in 1990 set the record as being the youngest female seed in the Ladies' Singles at Wimbledon?

WIMBLEDON - 1993

881. Who won the first of his many Wimbledon Men's Singles titles?

882. Can you recall the USA Runner-Up in the Men's Singles?

883. What former Multiple Champion did the 1993 Champion beat in the Men's Singles Semi-Finals?

884. What former Multiple Champion did the 1993 Runner-Up beat in the Men's Singles Semi-Finals?

885. Who won the Ladies' Singles title?

886. Name the losing Finalist from Czechoslovakia, and future Wimbledon Ladies' Singles Champion, in the Ladies' Singles.

887. Can you name the player, and future Wimbledon Ladies' Singles Champion, who lost her Semi-Final match in the Ladies' Singles to the eventual Champion?

888. Name either of the winning pair who won the first of many Wimbledon Men's Doubles titles.

889. Can you name either of the winning pair in the Ladies' Doubles who claimed their second of four titles?

890. Name either of the winning pair in the Mixed Doubles. The male player won his second Wimbledon title whilst the female player was a former Ladies' Singles Multiple Champion.

THE MEN'S GAME

891. Who in 1969 set the record as being the oldest male seed in the Men's Singles at Wimbledon?

892. Can you name the Swiss player who along with Martina Navratilova lost the 1986 Wimbledon Mixed Doubles Final?

893. Can you name the Australian player who along with Mrs A Neiland of the Netherlands lost the 1996 Wimbledon Mixed Doubles Final?

894. In what year was Jimmy Connors Runner-Up in the Australian Open - 1973, 1975 or 1977?

895. Who in 1992 was the last player to beat John McEnroe in a Men's Singles match at Wimbledon when he defeated him in the Semi-Finals?

896. Up to the end of 2004, who lay in 5th place in the Men's List of most number of weeks spent as the No. 1 ranked player in the world with 109?

897. What European player in 1973 won the French and Italian Opens in succession?

898. Name the American who beat Tom Okker in the 1968 US Open Final.

899. In what Men's Singles "Open" Final did Jan Kodes reach the Final of in 1970, 1971 & 1972 only to lose all 3?

900. Who won the ATP Most Improved Player Award for 1981 - Pat Cash, Ivan Lendl or Michael Stich?

THE LADIES' GAME

901. Who in 1971, at the time, became the youngest Ladies' US Open Single Semi-Finalist aged 16?

902. What "Catarina" did Martina Navratilova beat in the 1989 Wimbledon Ladies' Singles Semi-Final?

903. Martina Navratilova beat this player in the 1985 Ladies' Singles Quarter-Finals and the two of them went on to lose the 1985 Ladies' Doubles title at Wimbledon. Name her.

904. Can you name the Australian player that won the US Indoor title in 1973 by beating Virginia Wade 6-4, 6-4?

905. Name the British player who played in 26 Wimbledon tournaments, the last one in 1987.

906. Who won the Ladies' US Open title in 1964 - Maria Bueno, Billie Jean King or Margaret Smith?

907. In 1988 Steffi Graf won the Grand Slam. Name any opponent she beat in 1 of the 4 Finals.

908. Apart from the Grand Slam in 1988, what other Major Tennis Tournament did Steffi Graf win?

909. Of what Team was Tracey Austin a winning member in 1979 & 1981?

910. In 1963 two ladies were involved in the longest singles set played by women when they met in a Wightman Cup set lasting 36 games. Name either of the 2 players.

WIMBLEDON - 1994

911. Who won his second Men's Singles title?

912. Can you recall the Runner-Up, and future Wimbledon Men's Singles Champion, in the Men's Singles?

913. What "Todd" did the 1994 Champion beat in the Men's Singles Semi-Finals?

914. What former Multiple Men's Singles Champion did the 1994 Runner-Up beat in the Men's Singles Semi-Finals?

915. Can you name the Spanish player who won the Ladies' Singles title?

916. Name the losing Finalist in the Ladies' Singles which also marked her last appearance in a Ladies' Singles Final at Wimbledon.

917. Can you name the "Gigi" or "Lori" who both lost their Semi-Final matches in the Ladies' Singles?

918. Name either of the winning pair in the Men's Doubles who claimed their second Men's Doubles title at Wimbledon.

919. Can you name either of the Runners-Up, from Czechoslovakia and Spain, in the Ladies' Doubles Final?

920. Name either of the winning pair, from Australia and Czechoslovakia, in the Mixed Doubles.

MEN'S CHAMPIONS

921. Name the male Swedish player who is the 5-time recipient of the ATP's Sportsmanship Award, winning it more times than any other player.

922. Only 2 players have been ranked the No. 1 player in the world for more weeks in total than Jimmy Connors. Name either of the 2.

923. For how many consecutive weeks was Jimmy Connors ranked the No. 1 player in the world - 160, 170 or 180?

924. Can you name the American player who won the 1970 Australian Men's Singles?

925. What is John McEnroe's middle name?

926. Who in 1976 was the first European player to earn more than $1 million in career prize money?

927. How many Men's Doubles Finals did Jan Kodes reach - 7, 8 or 9?

928. Name the USA Davis Cup player who played in 12 Davis Cups in 1978-84, 1987-89, 1991 & 1992.

929. In 1956 Lew Hoad just missed out on achieving the Grand Slam winning 3 of the 4 Majors that year. Can you recall the one that eluded him in 1956?

930. How many times was Boris Becker named the ATP Player of the Year?

LADIES' CHAMPIONS

931. Name the female player who was the first player to win more than 150 tournaments.

932. In how many years did Billie Jean King win her 20 Wimbledon titles - 19, 21 or 23?

933. Can you name the Australian player who partnered Virginia Wade to Doubles success in the Australian, French and US Opens?

934. Name any 1 of the 4 women who in 1968 signed a Pro contract to tour in a female tournament group when they formed part of the women's auxiliary of the National Tennis League.

935. Who was the Wimbledon Ladies' Singles Champion from 1991 to 1993?

936. Name the British player who holds the record for competing in the most Federation Cups with 18 to her name.

937. Name the Australian player who won the Ladies' Doubles title at the Australian Open in 1971, 1974, 1975, 1976 & 1977.

938. Name the player that won the 1986 Virginia Slims Ladies' Singles Championships.

939. Who won the 1987 Ladies' Singles title at the French Open?

940. How many consecutive Wimbledon Ladies' Doubles titles did Martina Navratilova & Pam Shriver win during the 1980s?

WIMBLEDON - 1995

941. Who won the Men's Singles title?

942. Can you recall the Runner-Up in the Men's Singles which also marked his last appearance in the Wimbledon Men's Singles Final?

943. What future Wimbledon Champion did the 1995 Champion beat in the Men's Singles Semi-Finals?

944. What former American Wimbledon Men's Singles Champion did the 1995 Runner-Up beat in the Men's Singles Semi-Finals?

945. Who won the Ladies' Singles title?

946. Can you name the Spanish player who was the losing Finalist in the Ladies' Singles?

947. Can you name the future Wimbledon Ladies' Singles Champion who lost her Semi-Final match in the Ladies' Singles to the 1995 Champion?

948. Name either of the winning Australian pair in the Men's Doubles.

949. Can you name either of the winning pair, and former Runners-Up, in the Ladies' Doubles.

950. Name the female member of the winning pair in the Mixed Doubles who won the third of her four Wimbledon Mixed Doubles titles.

LEGEND - MARTINA NAVRATILOVA

951. How many Ladies' Singles titles did Martina win at Wimbledon?

952. Name any 3 of the years in which Martina won the Wimbledon Ladies' Singles title.

953. Who did Martina beat to win her first Wimbledon Ladies' Singles title?

954. In what city in Czechoslovakia was Martina born?

955. Can you name the Spanish player who beat Martina in her last Wimbledon Ladies' Singles Final in 1994?

956. How many Wimbledon titles did Martina win - 18, 19 or 20?

957. Excluding Wimbledon, what Grand Slam Singles title did Martina win the most?

958. Of the 17 tournaments she entered in 1983, how many did she win?

959. With what player did Martina win the Doubles Grand Slam of all 4 Majors in 1984?

960. In what year was Martina ranked the No. 1 player in the world for the first time in her career?

FIRST SET

961. Who was considered to be a "non-person" in the country of her birth for a number of years from 1975 onwards with even her exploits in tennis not appearing in the media of her homeland?

962. Who in 1968 became the only player in the history of tennis to have won both the US Amateur and US Open Championships in the same year?

963. Which 1 of the 4 Grand Slam Doubles Finals was the only one Virginia Wade failed to win?

964. Who was nicknamed the Bucharest Buffoon during his playing career?

965. Name the former 3-times South American-born Wimbledon Ladies' Singles Champion who won the 1974 Japan Open, her first and only Singles tournament victory as a Professional.

966. Can you name the Mexican player who along with Miss J S Newberry of the USA lost the 1973 Wimbledon Mixed Doubles Final?

967. Who was named the "Greatest Woman Athlete of the Last 25 Years" by the Women's Sports Foundation in 1985?

968. Can you name either of the 2 brothers who met in the 1991 Chicago Tennis Final?

969. Name the player who led her country to Federation Cup Team success in 1971, 1973 & 1974 and Runners-Up spot in 1975 & 1976.

970. Name the player who spent 157 straight weeks at No. 1 in the ATP Singles ratings between 1985-1988.

WIMBLEDON - 1996

971. What Dutch player won the Men's Singles title?

972. Can you recall the "Washington" that finished Runner-Up in the Men's Singles?

973. What "Jason" did the 1996 Champion beat in the Men's Singles Semi-Finals?

974. Name the "Martin" who lost his Semi-Final match to the eventual Runner-Up in the Men's Singles.

975. Who won the Ladies' Singles title?

976. Name the losing Finalist, for the second time in her career, in the Ladies Singles.

977. Can you name the future Wimbledon Ladies' Singles Champion that the 1996 Champion beat in the Last 16?

978. Name either of the winning pair in the Men's Doubles.

979. Can you name either of the winning pair in the Ladies' Doubles representing Czechoslovakia and Switzerland?

980. Name either of the winning pair in the Mixed Doubles, one of them winning their second Wimbledon title of 1996.

SECOND SET

981. In how many consecutive Wimbledon Ladies' Singles Finals did Martina Navratilova appear from 1982?

982. Name the youngest player to have won a Wimbledon Final.

983. What was the occupation of Chris Evert's father - Football Coach, Golf Coach or Tennis Coach?

984. Who holds the record for the most participations in the Davis Cup for the USA with 12 years?

985. In how many Wimbledon Finals did Billie Jean King appear - 26, 27 or 28?

986. Can you recall the American player that prevented Ilie Nastase from winning 4 consecutive Masters titles in 1974?

987. Can you name the British player who played in 21 Wightman Cups between 1965-1985?

988. What non-American in 1973 won 15 Men's Singles and 8 Men's Doubles titles?

989. Name the female player who has a record of 20-0 in Singles matches and 17-0 in Doubles matches in the Federation Cup.

990. Can you recall the European player who was named the ATP Most Improved Player of the Year for 1985?

WIMBLEDON - 1997

991. Who won the Men's Singles title?

992. Can you recall the French Runner-Up in the Men's Singles?

993. Name the Multiple Men's Doubles Champion that the 1997 Wimbledon Men's Singles Champion beat in the Semi-Finals?

994. What German player did the 1997 Wimbledon Men's Singles Runner-Up beat in the Semi-Finals?

995. What Swiss player won the Ladies' Singles title?

996. Name the future Wimbledon Ladies' Singles Champion who lost her second Wimbledon Ladies' Singles Final in 1997.

997. Can you name the "Russian pin-up" who lost her Semi-Final match in the Ladies' Singles to the eventual Champion?

998. Name either of the winning pair in the Men's Doubles.

999. Can you name either of the winning pair in the Ladies' Doubles who won their fourth and final Wimbledon Ladies' Doubles title?

1000. Name either of the winning pair in the Mixed Doubles who claimed their second Wimbledon Mixed Doubles title together.

PAST MASTER - PETE SAMPRAS

1001. What was the first Grand Slam Singles title that Pete won?

1002. In what year did he win his first Grand Slam Singles title - 1990, 1991 or 1992?

1003. Can you name the fellow countryman he beat in the Final of Q1001?

1004. How many Men's Singles titles did he win at Wimbledon?

1005. Name any 3 years he ruled Wimbledon.

1006. Can you name the Australian player he beat to win his last Men's Singles titles at Wimbledon?

1007. How many Grand Slam Singles titles did Pete win during his career?

1008. Name either the last Grand Slam Singles title he won or the player he beat in the Final.

1009. Name any 3 years in which Pete won the US Open Men's Singles title.

1010. What was the only Grand Slam Singles title that Pete failed to win?

THE EARLY 1970s AT WIMBLEDON

1011. What Australian won the first Men's Singles title in the 1970s?

1012. Can you name the Australian that won the first Ladies' Singles title in the 1970s?

1013. Who appeared in her first Ladies' Singles Final in 1971?

1014. Name the American winner of the 1972 Men's Singles title.

1015. Can you recall the name of either member of the winning pair that won the Men's Doubles title in 1970 & 1974?

1016. Who was the first player to successfully defend her Ladies' Singles title in the 1970s?

1017. What Australian lost the Men's Singles title in 1970 & 1974?

1018. Can you recall the name of either member of the winning Romania/USA pair that won the Mixed Doubles title in 1970 & 1972?

1019. Who was the first player to successfully defend his Men's Singles title in the 1970s?

1020. Can you recall the name of either member of the winning pair that won the Ladies' Doubles title in 1970, 1971 & 1973?

WIMBLEDON - 1998

1021. What American player won the Men's Singles title?

1022. Can you recall the Runner-Up in the Men's Singles?

1023. Name the British player that the 1998 Wimbledon Men's Singles Champion beat in the Semi-Finals?

1024. What former Men's Singles Champion did the 1998 Wimbledon Men's Singles Runner-Up beat in the Semi-Finals?

1025. What Czechoslovakian player won the Ladies' Singles title?

1026. Name the French player who lost the 1998 Wimbledon Ladies' Singles Final.

1027. Can you name the former Wimbledon Ladies' Singles Champion who lost her Semi-Final match in the Ladies' Singles to the eventual Champion?

1028. Name either of the winning Dutch pair in the Men's Doubles Final that prevented Todd Woodbridge & Mark Woodforde from claiming their sixth Men's Doubles title.

1029. What was unusual about the winning pair in the Wimbledon Ladies' Doubles Final?

1030. Name either of the winning pair in the Mixed Doubles.

THIRD SET

1031. Can you name the player who appeared in 12 consecutive Ladies' Grand Slam Singles Finals between 1987-1990?

1032. Up to and including 2004, who was the last American to win the Wimbledon Men's Singles title?

1033. How many Doubles titles did Evonne Goolagong Cawley win - 9, 19 or 29?

1034. Which Major is the fourth one to be played during the year on the Tennis Circuit?

1035. Who was voted the Female Athlete of the Decade by the national Sports Review, AP & UPI, for the 1980s?

1036. Can you name the male player who won 11 of the 17 tournaments he entered in 1985?

1037. Who won the Ladies' Singles title at Wimbledon the year before one of the Williams sisters won the title?

1038. Name the American player who won 10 of the 22 tournaments he entered in 1968.

1039. Name the female player who was the first player to win more than 1,000 Singles Matches.

1040. Who in 1979 broke Rod Laver's and Ilie Nastase's record of 23 titles (Singles & Doubles) in a single season when he won 27 titles?

WIMBLEDON IN THE 1960s

1041. Can you name the Australian that won the Men's Singles title in 1961 and successfully defended it the following year?

1042. Name either of the Australian winning pair in the Men's Doubles in both 1968 & 1969.

1043. Who won the Ladies' Singles title in 3 consecutive years from 1966-1968?

1044. Name the player who won the Ladies' Doubles title in 1960, 1963, 1965 & 1966.

1045. Name the Australian who lost 3 consecutive Men's Singles Finals from 1963-1965.

1046. Name either of the 2 British players who contested the 1961 Ladies' Singles Final.

1047. Who won his fourth Men's Singles title in 1969?

1048. Can you recall the South American player who successfully defended her Ladies' Singles crown in 1960?

1049. Name the Spanish Men's Singles Champion of 1966.

1050. Name the British player who defeated Billie Jean King in the 1969 Ladies' Singles Final.

MEN'S GRAND SLAM SINGLES WINNERS

ALL YOU HAVE TO DO HERE IS ASSOCIATE THE PLAYER WITH THE TOTAL NUMBER OF GRAND SLAM SINGLES TITLES HE WON DURING HIS CAREER

1051.	Jimmy Connors	12
1052.	Roy Emerson	7
1053.	Boris Becker	8
1054.	Bjorn Borg	8
1055.	Jim Courier	11
1056.	Ivan Lendl	14
1057.	Rod Laver	6
1058.	Pete Sampras	8
1059.	Andre Agassi	4
1060.	John McEnroe	11

LADIES' GRAND SLAM SINGLES WINNERS

ALL YOU HAVE TO DO HERE IS ASSOCIATE THE PLAYER WITH THE TOTAL NUMBER OF GRAND SLAM SINGLES TITLES SHE WON DURING HER CAREER

1061.	Chris Evert Lloyd	9
1062.	Martina Navratilova	7
1063.	Martina Hingis	19
1064.	Billie Jean King	18
1065.	Maureen Connolly	5
1066.	Steffi Graf	9
1067.	Margaret Smith Court	18
1068.	Maria Bueno	10
1069.	Monica Seles	24
1070.	Helen Willis Moody	22

PAST MASTER - FRED PERRY

1071. In what city was Fred born - Scunthorpe, Stockport or Southampton?

1072. What was Fred's middle name - Cecil, John or William?

1073. How many times did Fred win the Men's Singles title at Wimbledon?

1074. Name any year he was the Men's Singles Champion at Wimbledon.

1075. How many times did he win the Australian Open Men's Singles?

1076. Fred narrowly missed out on claiming the Grand Slam in 1934. Which one of the 4 Majors did he fail to win?

1077. How many US Open Singles titles did he claim during his career?

1078. Following on from Q1077, name any year he was Champion.

1079. Prior to taking up tennis at the age of 18, at what other sport had Fred excelled, winning many competitions in it?

1080. What type of business did Fred get involved in after his tennis career ended?

ANDRE AGASSI

1081. In what American gambling city was Andre born?

1082. Can you recall the year in which Andre turned Professional - 1984, 1985 or 1986?

1083. In what sport did Andre's father participate at the 1948 & 1952 Olympic Games?

1084. Can you recall the Olympic Games in which Andre won a gold medal?

1085. Name the first Grand Slam Singles title he won.

1086. Following on from Q1085, in what year did he win the title - 1990, 1991 or 1992?

1087. On his way to winning his first Singles Grand Slam title he beat a former Champion in the Quarter-Finals and in the Semi-Finals. Name either player concerned.

1088. In what year did Andre become only the fifth player in history to win all 4 Grand Slam Singles titles at some point during his career?

1089. Can you recall the name of the famous Tennis School attended by Andre?

1090. Which 1 of the 4 Major Grand Slam Singles title has Andre won the most?

WIMBLEDON - 1999

1091. Can you recall the winner of the Men's Singles title?

1092. Can you name the American Runner-Up in the Men's Singles?

1093. Who lost his second successive Men's Singles Semi-Final?

1094. What future Australian 2-times Wimbledon Men's Singles Runner-Up did the 1999 Runner-Up beat in the Semi-Finals?

1095. Can you name the American player who won the Ladies' Singles title?

1096. Name the player, and former Multiple Ladies' Singles Champion, in the Ladies' Singles Final who appeared in her last Wimbledon Final.

1097. Can you name either of the 2 beaten Semi-Finalists in the Ladies' Singles?

1098. Name either of the winning pair representing India in the Men's Doubles.

1099. Can you name either of the winning USA pair in the Ladies' Doubles?

1100. Name either of the winning pair in the Mixed Doubles, one of whom won their second Wimbledon title during the 1999 tournament.

FOURTH SET

1101. Name either of the 2 ladies involved in the only ever Wimbledon Singles Championship to end in a tie-breaker when it occurred in 1980.

1102. In 1969 Rod Laver won the Grand Slam. Name any opponent he beat in 1 of the 4 Finals.

1103. Who in 1976 became the first female player to earn more than $1 million in prize money?

1104. On how many occasions was John McEnroe the USA's No. 1 ranked player - 5, 6 or 7?

1105. Name the player who has played the most number of games at Wimbledon.

1106. What male won the Australian Open in 1989 and successfully defended it the following year?

1107. What "Open" did Virginia Wade win on clay in 1971?

1108. What former tennis Professional entered the elections for Lord Mayor of Bucharest in 1996?

1109. Name the world's No. 3 ranked player who, in August 1999, became the highest ranked player ever to announce her retirement from tennis since computer rankings began.

1110. Name the player who was the USA No. 1 ranked male player in 1968 & 1975.

WIMBLEDON - 2000

1111. Who won the Men's Singles title?

1112. Can you recall the Australian Runner-Up in the Men's Singles?

1113. Name the Russian player who the 2000 Champion beat in the Semi-Finals.

1114. What former Wimbledon Men's Singles Champion did the 2000 Men's Singles Runner-Up beat in the Semi-Finals?

1115. Who won the first of her Wimbledon Ladies' Singles titles?

1116. Name the losing Finalist, and former Wimbledon Ladies' Singles Champion, in the Ladies' Singles.

1117. Can you name the future Wimbledon Ladies' Singles Champion who lost her Semi-Final match in the Ladies' Singles to the eventual Champion?

1118. Name either of the winning pair in the Men's Doubles.

1119. Name the winning "family" pair in the Ladies' Doubles.

1120. Name either of the losing "boyfriend & girlfriend" pair in the Mixed Doubles Final.

FACTS & TRIVIA - 3

1121. Who won the 1988 & 1995 Ladies' Singles titles at the French Open?

1122. How many times did Boris Becker win the Davis Cup as a player?

1123. Can you name the Australian player who won the 1973 Italian Open Ladies' Singles title?

1124. How many Amateur Singles titles did Arthur Ashe win during his career - 25, 35 or 45?

1125. Who won the World Championship of Tennis Men's Singles in 1988 - Boris Becker, Stefan Edberg or Ivan Lendl?

1126. Can you name the Wimbledon Champion who was the President of the WTA from 1975-1976 and 1983-1991?

1127. Can you name the Swedish player who won the 1992 Men's Singles title at the US Open?

1128. Who did Chris Evert beat in the Final of the Ladies' Singles at the 1985 French Open?

1129. Can you name the American player won the 1995 Men's Singles title at the US Open?

1130. Can you name the American player won the 1974 Men's Singles title at the US Open?

WIMBLEDON - 2001

1131. Name the former Multiple Runner-Up who won the 2001 Men's Singles title.

1132. Can you recall the Australian Runner-Up in the Men's Singles?

1133. Name the crowd favourite that the 2001 Champion beat in the Semi-Finals.

1134. What former Multiple Grand Slam Singles Champion did the 2001 Men's Singles Runner-Up beat in the Semi-Finals?

1135. Who won the Ladies Singles title?

1136. Name the losing Finalist from Belgium in the Ladies' Singles Final.

1137. Can you name the former Wimbledon Ladies' Singles Champion who lost her Semi-Final match in the Ladies' Singles to the eventual Champion?

1138. Name either of the winning American pair in the Men's Doubles.

1139. Name the future winners of the Ladies' Doubles who were Runners-Up in the 2001 Ladies' Doubles Final.

1140. Name either of the winning Czechoslovakian/Slovakian pairing in the Mixed Doubles Final.

PAST MASTER - MATS WILANDER

1141. In 1987 Mats played in the longest ever US Open Men's Singles Final lasting 4 hours & 47 minutes. Name his opponent.

1142. Which 1 of the 4 Grand Slams was the only one Mats failed to capture?

1143. Which 1 of the 4 Grand Slams was the first one he won?

1144. Following on from Q1143, in what year did he triumph?

1145. Overall how many Grand Slam Singles titles did he win?

1146. Can you recall the American player who beat Mats in a 5-set 1982 Davis Cup tie that lasted a remarkable 6 hours & 32 minutes?

1147. Name any year in which Mats won the Australian Open Men's Singles title.

1148. What Award did he win in 1988?

1149. Can you recall the highest ever world ranking he achieved?

1150. Can you name the former No. 1 ranked player in the world and winner of the 2000 US Open that Mat has coached?

WIMBLEDON - 2002

1151. Name the Australian who won the 2002 Men's Singles title.

1152. Can you recall the Argentinian Runner-Up in the Men's Singles?

1153. Who put Tim Henman out of the tournament?

1154. Name the "Xavier" that the eventual Runner-Up beat in the Semi-Finals.

1155. Who won her first Ladies' Singles title?

1156. Name the losing Finalist in the Ladies' Singles Final.

1157. Can you name the French player who lost her Semi-Final match in the Ladies' Singles to the eventual Champion?

1158. Name either of the players who won their first Wimbledon Men's Doubles title together.

1159. Name either member of the winning Ladies' Doubles team.

1160. Name either of the winning Indian/Russian pairing in the Mixed Doubles Final.

DEUCE

1161. Name either of the 2 players who were voted WTA Tour Doubles Team of the Year from 1981-1989.

1162. Who was the Runner-Up in the Men's Singles in the 1986 World Championship of Tennis - Boris Becker, Jim Courier or John McEnroe?

1163. Name the American who won the Wimbledon Ladies' Singles title in 3 consecutive years, 1952-1954.

1164. What is Virginia Wade's middle name - Sally, Sarah or Stephanie?

1165. Who set a record of having won a Grand Slam Singles title in 13 consecutive years between 1974-1986?

1166. Name the Australian player that won 9 Ladies' Singles titles in 1973.

1167. Who won her first Ladies' US Open title in 1959 and her fourth in 1966?

1168. Name the Swedish player who took over as the No. 1 ranked player in the world from Ivan Lendl.

1169. Who was voted the Associated Press Female Athlete of the Year in 1983?

1170. In what Australian city was Lew Hoad born?

ADVANTAGE

1171. In 1972 he was one of the founders of the ATP, he served as ATP President and won 3 Grand Slam Men's Singles titles during his career. Who is he?

1172. Name the player who holds the record of 7 French Open Ladies' Singles titles.

1173. What was the occupation of Billie Jean King's father - Basketball Coach, Policeman or Fireman?

1174. Who won the 1983 Ladies' Singles title at the French Open?

1175. Can you name the American player that won the 1982 Men's Singles title at the US Open?

1176. Can you name the player that won the 1959 Men's Singles title at the US Open and retained his title the following year?

1177. How many Doubles titles did Boris Becker win during his career - 15, 20 or 25?

1178. How many Singles titles did Evonne Goolagong Cawley win - 43, 53 or 63?

1179. What female player was ranked No. 19 in ESPN's Sports Century Top 50 Athletes for 1999?

1180. Can you name the Australian winner of the US Open Men's Singles title in 1966 - Rod Laver, John Newcombe or Fred Stolle?

TIM HENMAN

1181. In what city was Tim born - Birmingham, London or Oxford?

1182. What type of "disease" was Tim diagnosed with when he was at school?

1183. What Championship did Tim win in 1992 in both the Singles and Doubles?

1184. Can you recall the year in which Tim joined the ATP Tour - 1993, 1994 or 1995?

1185. To what "Top" numbered ranking did Tim manage to gain entry in 1996 - 10, 20 or 30?

1186. What Award did Tim win in 1996?

1187. In what country did Tim win his first ATP Tour event?

1188. Can you recall the Awards Ceremony in which Tim was the Runner-Up for 1997?

1189. With what other tennis player does Tim share his birthday?

1190. Up to 2004, how many times has Tim reached the Semi-Finals at Wimbledon in the Men's Singles?

GAME, SET & MATCH

1191. Can you name the Swedish player who won the 1980 Men's Singles title at the French Open?

1192. Who holds the record of 101 match victories in the Ladies' Singles at the US Open?

1193. Who won the first of his 3 Men's Singles French Open titles in 1997?

1194. Who in 1988 prevented Martina Navratilova from winning her seventh consecutive Ladies' Singles title at Wimbledon?

1195. Who was the Runner-Up in the Masters Tournament on 3 occasions in 1985, 1986 & 1989?

1196. Name the only player to have lost 4 consecutive US Open Finals.

1197. Who in 1962 was the last British player to win the Boys' Singles Final at Wimbledon?

1198. What was the highest ever world ranking that Virginia Wade reached?

1199. Can you name the Wimbledon Men's Singles Champion from the 1970's that captained the USA Davis Cup team from 1981-1985?

1200. How many Doubles, including Mixed Doubles, titles did Billie Jean King win at Wimbledon?

EXPERT - PAST MASTER - JIMMY CONNORS

1201. Jimmy won 109 Singles titles, but how many times was he a beaten Finalist - 54, 74 or 94?

1202. Where in the USA was Jimmy born?

1203. In what year did Jimmy win his first Professional tournament?

1204. In what Middle East country did Jimmy win his record 109th Men's Singles competition?

1205. What 3 Majors did Jimmy win in 1974?

1206. On how many occasions did Jimmy represent the USA in the Davis Cup?

1207. Name any year Jimmy played for the USA in the Davis Cup.

1208. What Singles title did Jimmy win in 1971?

1209. In 1973 Jimmy was ranked joint-No. 1 in the world with a fellow American. Name him.

1210. How many times during his 21 years as a Professional was Jimmy ranked in the world's Top 10 players?

EXPERT - MEN'S SINGLES CHAMPION

ALL YOU HAVE TO DO HERE IS ASSOCIATE THE PLAYER WITH THE YEAR HE WON THE MEN'S SINGLES TITLE AT WIMBLEDON

1211.	Lew Hoad	1962
1212.	Roy Emerson	1963
1213.	Rod Laver	1958
1214.	Neale Fisher	1959
1215.	Frank Sedgman	1964
1216.	Jaroslav Drobny	1960
1217.	Ashley Cooper	1966
1218.	Chuck McKinley	1956
1219.	Alex Olmedo	1954
1220.	Manuel Santana	1952

EXPERT - LADIES' SINGLES CHAMPION

ALL YOU HAVE TO DO HERE IS ASSOCIATE THE PLAYER WITH THE YEAR SHE WON THE LADIES' SINGLES TITLE AT WIMBLEDON

1221.	Maria Bueno	1956
1222.	Karen Hantze (Susman)	1966
1223.	Louise Brough	1951
1224.	Billie Jean King	1958
1225.	Angela Mortimer	1955
1226.	Margaret Smith	1953
1227.	Althea Gibson	1962
1228.	Shirley Fry	1961
1229.	Maureen Connolly	1964
1230.	Doris Hart	1965

EXPERT - WIMBLEDON 2004

1231. A former Ladies' Singles Champion was knocked out in the 1st Round. Name her.

1232. What seeding was Tim Henman given?

1233. What seeding was Maria Sharapova, the Ladies' Singles Champion, awarded for the tournament?

1234. Roger Federer beat a former Champion in the Quarter-Finals. Name him.

1235. Can you name the Ladies' French No. 24 seed that was knocked out in the 1st Round?

1236. Name the unseeded player who progressed the furthest in the Men's Singles.

1237. Name the unseeded player who progressed the furthest in the Ladies' Singles.

1238. Can you name the Japanese player who made it to the Quarter-Finals in the Ladies' Singles?

1239. Maria Sharapova beat a former Champion on her way to winning the Ladies' Singles. Can you name her?

1240. Name the Dutch player who made it as far as the Quarter-Finals in the Men's Singles.

EXPERT - BJORN BORG

1241. In what year was Bjorn born?

1242. What is his middle name?

1243. In what part of Sweden was Bjorn born?

1244. In 1973 Bjorn became the youngest winner of the French Open. Can you name his fellow countryman that beat this record when he won the French Open in 1982?

1245. Apart from the French Open in 1975, what other competition did he win that year?

1246. During his Professional career, who did Bjorn play 14 times in competition, winning and losing 7 games?

1247. How many times did Bjorn win the French Open title?

1248. In what year did he win his last Major?

1249. Whose record of 31 games won at Wimbledon in the Men's Singles did Bjorn surpass during the 1980 Championships?

1250. Can you recall the American player who Bjorn beat in a thrilling 5-set Semi-Final at Wimbledon in 1977?

EXPERT - MEN'S DOUBLES CHAMPIONS

ALL YOU HAVE TO DO HERE IS ASSOCIATE THE PLAYERS WITH THE YEAR THEY WON THE MEN'S DOUBLES TITLE AT WIMBLEDON

1251.	1977	P McNamara & P McNamee (AUS)
1252.	1976	H Gunthardt (SWI) & B Taroczy (HUN)
1253.	1975	J Newcombe & A Roche (AUS)
1254.	1982	R Hewitt & F McMillan (SA)
1255.	1979	R Emerson & R Laver (AUS)
1256.	1985	P Fleming & J McEnroe (USA)
1257.	1973	B Gottfried (USA) & R Ramirez (MEX)
1258.	1972	J Connors (USA) & I Nastase (ROM)
1259.	1971	R Case & G Masters (AUS)
1260.	1970	V Gerulaitis & A Mayer (USA)

EXPERT - MEN'S ATP FINAL RANKINGS FOR 2004

ALL YOU HAVE TO DO HERE IS ASSOCIATE THE PLAYER WITH HIS ATP RANKING AT THE END OF THE 2004 SEASON

1261.	S Grosjean	17
1262.	G Canas	13
1263.	N Kiefer	14
1264.	M Youzhny	12
1265.	D Hrbaty	11
1266.	J Johansson	18
1267.	T Robredo	19
1268.	V Spadea	15
1269.	T Haas	20
1270.	N Massu	16

EXPERT - LADIES' WTP FINAL RANKINGS FOR 2004

ALL YOU HAVE TO DO HERE IS ASSOCIATE THE PLAYER WITH HER WTP RANKING AT THE END OF THE 2004 SEASON

1271.	S F'ina-Elia	18
1272.	A Sugiyama	19
1273.	N Petrova	14
1274.	A Molik	15
1275.	F Schiavone	13
1276.	P Suarez	10
1277.	V Zvonareva	16
1278.	E Bovina	17
1279.	K Sprem	12
1280.	P Schnyder	11

EXPERT - IVAN LENDL

1281. How many times did Ivan win the ATP Player of the Year Award?

1282. Name any year in which Ivan won the ATP Player of the Year Award.

1283. Name either of the 2 players with whom Ivan shares the Grand Prix record of 15 wins in a year.

1284. Where in Czechoslovakia was Ivan born?

1285. In what year did he become a US citizen?

1286. How many Grand Slam titles did Ivan win during his career?

1287. In how many Grand Slam Singles Finals did he appear?

1288. How many consecutive US Open Finals did Ivan reach during the 1980s?

1289. In 1982 Ivan won 15 tournaments. In how many had he actually participate - 19, 21 or 23?

1290. What competition did he win in 1980?

EXPERT - MEN'S ATP FINAL RANKINGS FOR 1997

ALL YOU HAVE TO DO HERE IS ASSOCIATE THE PLAYER WITH HIS ATP RANKING AT THE END OF THE 1997 SEASON

1291.	Albert Costa	16
1292.	Goran Ivanisevic	17
1293.	Tim Henman	13
1294.	Richard Krajicek	18
1295.	Felix Mantilla	14
1296.	Alex Corretja	20
1297.	Mark Philippoussis	12
1298.	Petr Korda	19
1299.	Gustavo Kurten	11
1300.	Cedric Pioline	15

EXPERT - LEGEND - BILLIE JEAN KING

1301. To the nearest 5, how many Amateur titles did Billie Jean win?

1302. In what non-Major did Billie Jean win both the Singles and Doubles in 1970?

1303. What Cup did Billie Jean win 10 times in 1961-67, 1970, 1977 & 1978?

1304. How many times was Billie Jean the non-playing Captain of the USA's Federation Cup Team?

1305. Name any year in which Billie Jean was the non-playing Captain of the USA's Federation Cup Team.

1306. What Mixed Doubles Major did Billie Jean win in 1968?

1307. In what year did she win her first Wimbledon Singles title?

1308. Who did Billie Jean beat to win her sixth and last Wimbledon Ladies' Singles title?

1309. Name either of the 2 years in which Billie Jean won the Wimbledon Singles, Doubles and Mixed Doubles titles.

1310. To the nearest 5, in how many Finals did Billie Jean finish Runner-Up during her Professional career?

EXPERT - THE NEARLY MEN

ALL YOU HAVE TO DO HERE IS ASSOCIATE THE PLAYER WITH THE YEAR HE LOST THE MEN'S SINGLES FINAL AT WIMBLEDON

1311.	Jimmy Connors	1969
1312.	Ken Rosewall	1986
1313.	Roscoe Tanner	1974
1314.	Ilie Nastase	1983
1315.	John Newcombe	1981
1316.	Boris Becker	1978
1317.	Bjorn Borg	1976
1318.	Stan Smith	1990
1319.	Ivan Lendl	1971
1320.	Chris Lewis	1979

EXPERT - THE NEARLY WOMEN

ALL YOU HAVE TO DO HERE IS ASSOCIATE THE PLAYER WITH THE YEAR SHE LOST THE LADIES' SINGLES FINAL AT WIMBLEDON

1321.	Arantxa Sanchez-Vicario	1990
1322.	Lindsay Davenport	1978
1323.	Martina Navratilova	1987
1324.	Evonne Cawley	1992
1325.	Gabriela Sabatini	1976
1326.	Chris Evert	1994
1327.	Monica Seles	1983
1328.	Steffi Graf	1991
1329.	Andrea Jaeger	2000
1330.	Zina Garrison	1996

EXPERT - MEN'S US OPEN CHAMPIONS

ALL YOU HAVE TO DO HERE IS ASSOCIATE THE PLAYER WITH THE YEAR HE WON THE MEN'S US OPEN

1331.	John Newcombe	1979
1332.	Jimmy Connors	1970
1333.	Rod Laver	1975
1334.	Fred Stolle	1969
1335.	John McEnroe	1964
1336.	Roy Emerson	1973
1337.	Stan Smith	1965
1338.	Manuel Orantes	1966
1339.	Manuel Santana	1971
1340.	Ken Rosewall	1976

EXPERT - LADIES' US OPEN CHAMPIONS

ALL YOU HAVE TO DO HERE IS ASSOCIATE THE PLAYER WITH THE YEAR SHE WON THE LADIES' US OPEN

1341.	Martina Navratilova	1963
1342.	Chris Evert Lloyd	1956
1343.	Darlene Hard	1968
1344.	Shirley Fry	1980
1345.	Margaret Smith Court	1958
1346.	Virginia Wade	1988
1347.	Althea Gibson	1970
1348.	Billie Jean King	1986
1349.	Maria Bueno	1967
1350.	Steffi Graf	1961

EXPERT - THE AUSTRALIAN OPEN

1351. What is the name of the Cup that is awarded to the winner of the Men's Singles title in the Australian Open?

1352. In what year did the Australian Open move to Melbourne on a permanent basis - 1972, 1975 or 1978?

1353. What "Ace" name is given to the surface on which the Australian Open is played?

1354. What is the name of the Cup that is awarded to the winner of the Ladies' Singles title in the Australian Open?

1355. Can you name the male tennis player who presented the Men's Singles trophy to the winner of the Centenary Australian Open in 2004?

1356. How many times did the player in Q1355 win the Men's Singles title in the Australian Open?

1357. Can you name the female tennis player who presented the Ladies' Singles trophy to the winner of the Centenary Australian Open in 2004?

1358. How many times did the player in Q1357 win the Ladies' Singles title in the Australian Open?

1359. Who in 2004 played her last match at the Australian Open, losing in the Mixed Doubles Final?

1360. Can you name the Scandinavian player who won the first Australian Open Men's Singles competition at its new Melbourne Park home in 1988?

EXPERT - MEN'S FRENCH OPEN CHAMPIONS

ALL YOU HAVE TO DO HERE IS ASSOCIATE THE PLAYER WITH THE YEAR HE WON THE MEN'S FRENCH OPEN

1361.	Bjorn Borg	1966
1362.	Ilie Nastase	1962
1363.	Guillermo Vilas	1982
1364.	Andres Gimeno	1963
1365.	Ken Rosewall	1977
1366.	Mats Wilander	1975
1367.	Adriano Panatta	1968
1368.	Roy Emerson	1972
1369.	Tony Roche	1973
1370.	Rod Laver	1976

EXPERT - LADIES' FRENCH OPEN CHAMPIONS

ALL YOU HAVE TO DO HERE IS ASSOCIATE THE PLAYER WITH THE YEAR SHE WON THE LADIES' FRENCH OPEN

1371.	Steffi Graf	1968
1372.	Arantxa Sanchez-Vicario	1973
1373.	Chris Evert Lloyd	1971
1374.	Virginia Ruzici	1966
1375.	Evonne Goolagong	1993
1376.	Margaret Smith Court	1986
1377.	Monica Seles	1967
1378.	Ann Haydon Jones	1978
1379.	Nancy Richey	1991
1380.	Françoise Durr	1998

EXPERT - PAST MASTER - BORIS BECKER

1381. Can you name the player that Boris played in 3 consecutive Wimbledon Men's Singles Finals from 1988-1990?

1382. Who did Boris beat in the Final of the 1986 Wimbledon Men's Singles Final to retain his title?

1383. How many sets were played in the Final when Boris beat Kevin Curren to win his first Wimbledon title in 1985?

1384. What was the only Grand Slam tournament that Boris failed to win?

1385. Following on from Q1384, how many times was Boris a Semi-Finalist in the competition?

1386. In what year was Boris ranked the No. 1 player in the world for the first time?

1387. How many Singles titles did Boris win during his Professional career?

1388. Where in Germany was Boris born?

1389. What Championship did Boris win in 1992 & 1995?

1390. Who did Boris beat in the Semi-Final of the 1995 Men's Singles at Wimbledon after falling a set behind?

EXPERT - 2004 CHAMPIONS TOUR RANKINGS

ALL YOU HAVE TO DO HERE IS ASSOCIATE THE PLAYER WITH HIS RANKING

1391.	Richard Krajicek	Joint 16th
1392.	Goran Ivanisevic	Joint 20th
1393.	Omar Camporese	Joint 16th
1394.	Petr Korda	9th
1395.	Paolo Cane	11th
1396.	Alex Antonitsch	13th
1397.	Cedric Pioline	8th
1398.	Emilio Sanchez	Joint 20th
1399.	Joao Cunha Silva	4th
1400.	Michael Stich	Joint 16th

EXPERT - 2003 CHAMPIONS TOUR RANKINGS

ALL YOU HAVE TO DO HERE IS ASSOCIATE THE PLAYER WITH HIS RANKING

1401.	Michael Stich	15th
1402.	Henri Leconte	9th
1403.	John McEnroe	Joint 13th
1404.	Pat Cash	Joint 20th
1405.	Cedric Pioline	17th
1406.	Thierry Champion	Joint 11th
1407.	Emilio Sanchez	10th
1408.	Yannick Noah	3rd
1409.	Jeremy Bates	1st
1410.	Felip Dewulf	5th

EXPERT - WIMBLEDON RECORDS

1411. The USA holds the record for providing the most Men's Singles Champions. Up to the 2004 tournament, how many Men's Champions were from the USA?

1412. The USA holds the record for providing the most Ladies' Singles Champions. Up to the 2004 tournament, how many Ladies' Champions were from the USA?

1413. How many Ladies' Doubles Championships did Elizabeth Ryan win?

1414. Name the player who holds the Ladies' record for the most number of Mixed Doubles titles.

1415. Can you name any 1 of the 3 male players who jointly hold the record of 3 Mixed Doubles titles each?

1416. Apart from Sweden, can you name the other country that has provided a total of 7 Men's Singles winners?

1417. Name the female USA player who holds the record of the youngest Mixed Doubles winner.

1418. Can you name the European player who holds the record of being the youngest ever Ladies' Doubles winner?

1419. Name the player who holds the record of being the oldest ever Mixed Doubles winner.

1420. Who was the last female player to win the Singles, Doubles & Mixed Doubles at Wimbledon in the same year?

EXPERT - WIMBLEDON LADIES' DOUBLES WINNERS

ALL YOU HAVE TO DO HERE IS ASSOCIATE THE WINNING PARTNERSHIP WITH THE YEAR THEY WON THE LADIES' DOUBLES AT WIMBLEDON

1421.	Miss L M Raymond & Miss R P Stubbs	1974
1422.	Miss B C Fernandez & Miss N M Zvereva	1981
1423.	Miss J Novotna & Miss H Sukova	1978
1424.	Mrs G E Reid & Miss W M Turnbull	2000
1425.	Miss M Navratilova & Miss P Shriver	1997
1426.	Miss R Casals & Mrs L W King	1980
1427.	Miss A K Kiyomura & Miss K Sawamatsu	2001
1428.	Miss E F Goolagong & Miss M S A Michel	1990
1429.	Miss V E S Williams & Miss S J Williams	1975
1430.	Miss K Jordan & Miss A E Smith	1973

EXPERT - LEGEND - STEFFI GRAF

1431. In what year did Steffi appear in her first Wimbledon Ladies' Singles Final?

1432. Name any year in which Steffi was the Runner-Up in the French Open Singles.

1433. Can you name any year in which Steffi was the Runner-Up in the US Open Singles?

1434. Who beat Steffi in her last Ladies' Singles Final at Wimbledon?

1435. To the nearest 50, how many weeks in total did Steffi spend as the No. 1 ranked player in the world?

1436. To the nearest 10, how many consecutive weeks was Steffi ranked the No. 1 player in the world, setting a record in doing so?

1437. On how many occasions was Steffi awarded the WTA Player of the Year Award?

1438. Following on from Q1437, name any 3 of the years she won the Award.

1439. What Championship did Steffi win 7 times in 1987-1990, 1993, 1995 & 1996?

1440. How many Olympic Games medals did Steffi win during her career?

EXPERT - PAST MASTER - JOHN McENROE

1441. What was the first Grand Slam competition he won?

1442. To whom did John lose in the Men's Singles Semi-Finals at his first Wimbledon?

1443. At what "Open" in 1990 was he disqualified for directing abusive language to Court Officials while leading Mikael Pernfors at the time?

1444. How many times did John win the US Open Men's Singles title?

1445. Following on from Q1444, name any 2 of the years he was Champion.

1446. With whom did John win 4 Men's Doubles with at Wimbledon?

1447. Name any year in which John won the Wimbledon Men's Doubles title.

1448. Who was John playing at Wimbledon in 1981 when he referred to an Umpire as "the pits of the world"?

1449. Following on from Q1448, can you name either the Umpire or the Referee?

1450. What Grand Slam Junior Singles title did he win in 1977?

EXPERT - LEGEND - CHRIS EVERT LLOYD

1451. How many times did Chris win the Ladies' Singles title at the Australian Open?

1452. Name any year in which Chris won the Ladies' Singles title at the Australian Open.

1453. In what year did Chris win her first Ladies' Singles title at the French Open?

1454. Who ended Chris's 55-match unbeaten run in 1974?

1455. Name any 3 of the 5 years in which she was the No. 1 ranked player in the world.

1456. How many Grand Slam Finals did Chris win during her career?

1457. What was the last Grand Slam Final that Chris won?

1458. Can you name the only Grand Slam tournament in which Chris failed to reach the Final at least once in the Ladies' Doubles?

1459. Of the 57 Major Grand Slam tournaments that Chris entered, how many times did she reach at least the Semi-Finals?

1460. What player did Chris beat in both the 1975 US Open and the 1976 Wimbledon Finals?

EXPERT - LEGEND - MARTINA NAVRATILOVA

1461. Who did Martina Navratilova beat in the 1990 Final to claim her record ninth Wimbledon Ladies' Singles title?

1462. How many times did Martina win the Ladies' Singles at the US Open?

1463. Name any year in which she won the Ladies' Singles at the French Open.

1464. What player did Martina play in 3 consecutive Wimbledon Ladies' Singles Finals?

1465. To the nearest 25, how many weeks in total was Martina the No. 1 ranked player in the world?

1466. On how many occasions was Martina voted the WTA Player of the Year?

1467. Name Martina's Doubles partner when they were named the 1977 WTA Tour Doubles Team of the Year.

1468. Martina won her record-equalling 20th Wimbledon title in 2003. In what event did she win it?

1469. To the nearest 10, how many Singles titles did Martina win during her career?

1470. To the nearest 10, how many Doubles titles did Martina win during her career?

EXPERT - MIXED SETS - 1

1471. Can you recall who was named the ATP Player of the Year in 1989?

1472. In what year was Virginia Wade first ranked in the world's Top 10?

1473. Name the American that won the USA Intercollegiate Men's Singles & Doubles titles in 1965.

1474. What brother and sister pair lost the 1981 Wimbledon Mixed Doubles Final?

1475. Can you name the player who appeared in all 11 Ladies' Grand Slam Singles Finals between 1985-1987?

1476. Was the first Australian Open staged at a Bowling Club, Cricket Club or Rugby Club?

1477. Who did Jan Kodes beat to win his first French Open in 1970?

1478. Can you name the player who won all 4 Major Ladies' Doubles titles in 1960 and the Wimbledon Singles crown?

1479. Name either member of the successful Australian Davis Cup Doubles pairing that helped Australia win the Cup in 1965 & 1967.

1480. What was the surname of the 2 sisters who in 1974 became the first sisters since Ethel (2) & Florence (3) Sutton to be ranked in the USA's Top 10 players' rankings?

EXPERT - FACTS & TRIVIA

1481. Can you name either of the 2 brothers who in the 1987 Madrid Tennis Final became the first pair of brothers to meet in a Professional Tennis Final?

1482. In how many consecutive Wimbledon Ladies' Doubles Finals did Martina Navratilova & Pam Shriver appear during the 1980s?

1483. In 1973 Billie Jean King took part in a "Battle of the Sexes" tennis challenge match. Who did she play?

1484. In what year did Lew Hoad win the first of his Men's Singles titles at Wimbledon?

1485. Can you name the non-American player who played World Team Tennis for Hawaii in 1976 and Los Angeles in 1977 & 1978, leading Los Angeles to the 1978 League Championship as their Player-Coach?

1486. Who has a Davis Cup Career Record of 53 wins and 12 defeats, 38-3 in Singles and 15-9 in Doubles?

1487. Who is the only player to have won each of the Grand Slam Singles titles on at least 4 occasions?

1488. Can you name either of the 2 sisters who played for the USA against Great Britain in the 1973 Wightman Cup?

1489. Who was the first unseeded player to win the Men's Singles title at Wimbledon?

1490. Name the male or female player that ended the 2001 season as the No. 1 ranked player in the world?

EXPERT - MIXED SETS - 2

1491. Who in 1987 won the triple of Ladies' Singles, Ladies' Doubles and Mixed Doubles at the US Open?

1492. In 1953 Maureen Connolly won the Grand Slam. Name any opponent she beat in 1 of the 4 Finals.

1493. What Singles title did Maria Bueno win in 1958, 1961 & 1965?

1494. Who in 1972 was the first man to beat Jan Kodes in the French Open Singles in 18 matches?

1495. At what Major did Jimmy Connors win the Men's Doubles Championship in 1975?

1496. Name the 2 players who were voted WTA Tour Doubles Team of the Year in 1978 & 1979.

1497. Who did Jan Kodes beat in the 1973 Wimbledon Men's Singles Final?

1498. In 1938 Donald Budge won the Grand Slam. Name any opponent he beat in 1 of the 4 Finals.

1499. Prior to Maria Sharapova's win in 2004, who was the last non-American to win the Ladies' Singles title at Wimbledon?

1500. Can you name the player who was the Grand Prix Masters Runner-Up in 1980, 1983, 1984 & 1988?

ANSWERS

MEN'S SINGLES CHAMPION - 1

1.	Lleyton Hewitt	2002
2.	John Newcombe	1971
3.	Jimmy Connors	1974
4.	John McEnroe	1981
5.	Bjorn Borg	1980
6.	Roger Federer	2003
7.	Goran Ivanisevic	2001
8.	Richard Krajicek	1996
9.	Jan Kodes	1973
10.	Pete Sampras	2000

LADIES' SINGLES CHAMPION - 1

11.	Serena Williams	2002
12.	Venus Williams	2001
13.	Maria Sharapova	2004
14.	Steffi Graf	1996
15.	Conchita Martinez	1994
16.	Martina Navratilova	1990
17.	Evonne Goolagong	1971
18.	Chris Evert	1976
19.	Virginia Wade	1977
20.	Billie Jean King	1973

WIMBLEDON - 1975

21. Arthur Ashe
22. Jimmy Connors
23. Tony Roche
24. Roscoe Tanner
25. Billie Jean King
26. Evonne Cawley
27. Chris Evert
28. Vitas Gerulaitis & A A Meyer
29. Miss A K Kiyomura & Miss K Sawamatsu
30. M C Riessen & Mrs B M Court

DAVIS CUP WINNERS - 1

31.	Great Britain	1935

32.	Australia	1977
33.	South Africa	1974
34.	France	2001
35.	Russia	2002
36.	Sweden	1975
37.	Czechoslovakia	1980
38.	USA	1978
39.	Germany	1989
40.	Italy	1976

PAST MASTER - JIMMY CONNORS

41. Scott
42. 2
43. 1974 & 1982
44. 4
45. 1975, 1977, 1978 & 1984
46. 109
47. 1972
48. Ken Rosewall
49. John McEnroe (1984)
50. 5

LEGEND - TRACEY AUSTIN

51. California (Palos Verdes)
52. Ann
53. US Under-12s
54. US Open
55. 1980
56. 2
57. US Open (1979 & 1981)
58. Italy
59. 1978
60. The USA Federation Cup Team

WIMBLEDON - 2004

61. Roger Federer
62. Andy Roddick
63. Mario Ancic & Sebastien Grojan
64. Maria Sharapova
65. Serena Williams
66. Lindsay Davenport & Amelie Mauresmo
67. Mario Ancic
68. Quarter-Finals

69. 2nd
70. Jennifer Capriati

PAST MASTER - BJORN BORG

71. 5
72. 1976
73. Ilie Nastase
74. John McEnroe
75. Jimmy Connors (1977 & 1978)
76. Roscoe Tanner (1979)
77. 4
78. The French Open
79. Fila
80. 62

WIMBLEDON - 2003

81. Roger Federer
82. Mark Philippoussis
83. Sebastien Grojan & Andy Roddick
84. Serena Williams
85. Venus Williams
86. Kim Clijsters & Justine Henin-Hardenne
87. 10th
88. Martina Navratilova (in the Mixed Doubles)
89. Andre Agassi
90. Todd Woodbridge (teamed up with Jonas Bjorkman)

WIMBLEDON - 1976

91. Bjorn Borg
92. Ilie Nastase
93. Roscoe Tanner
94. Raul Ramirez
95. Chris Evert
96. Evonne Cawley
97. Martina Navratilova
98. B E Gottfried & R C Ramirez
99. Miss C M Evert & Miss M Navratilova
100. A D Roche & Miss F D Durr

MEN'S ATP FINAL RANKINGS FOR 2004

101.	G Gaudio	10
102.	G Coria	7
103.	R Federer	1

104.	A Agassi	8
105.	D Nalbandian	9
106.	C Moya	5
107.	T Henman	6
108.	A Roddick	2
109.	M Safin	4
110.	L Hewitt	3

LADIES' WTP FINAL RANKINGS FOR 2004

111.	E Dementieva	6
112.	A Myskina	3
113.	J Capriati	10
114.	L Davenport	1
115.	M Sharapova	4
116.	V Williams	9
117.	A Mauresmo	2
118.	J Henin-Hardenne	8
119.	S Kuznetsova	5
120.	S Williams	7

PAST MASTER - IVAN LENDL

121. He never won it.
122. 2
123. 1986 & 1987
124. Boris Becker (1986) & Pat Cash (1987)
125. 4
126. 1985, 1986, 1987 & 1989
127. The French Open
128. 3
129. 1985, 1986 & 1987
130. The Grand Prix Masters

VENUS WILLIAMS

131. Richard Williams
132. 1994
133. The French Open
134. Wimbledon (2000)
135. She was the first woman to win a gold medal in Singles and a gold medal in Doubles (with sister Serena) at the Olympic Games (Sydney)
136. 1998 (IGA Tennis Classic)
137. Justine Henin-Hardenne
138. The Lipton Championships
139. 2 (2000 & 2001)

140. Lindsay Davenport

THE DAVIS CUP

141. 1900
142. India
143. Australia
144. USA
145. France
146. Sweden
147. 1978 (lost to the USA)
148. Russia
149. Germany (3-2)
150. Australia

WIMBLEDON - 1977

151. Bjorn Borg
152. Jimmy Connors
153. Vitas Gerulaitis
154. John McEnroe
155. Virginia Wade
156. Betty Stove
157. Chris Evert
158. R L Case & G Masters
159. Mrs R L Cawley & Miss J C Russell
160. R A J Hewitt & Miss G R Stevens

DAVIS CUP WINNERS - 2

161.	Australia	1973
162.	USA	1981
163.	Germany	1988
164.	Sweden	1985
165.	France	1991
166.	Spain	2000
167.	USA	1995
168.	Australia	1983
169.	Germany	1993
170.	Sweden	1987

LEGEND - BILLIE JEAN KING

171. Moffitt
172. The Women's Doubles (with Karen Hantze in 1961)
173. 20
174. Martina Navratilova

175.	6
176.	1975
177.	The USA Federation Cup Team
178.	Lindsay Davenport, Gigi Fernandez & Mary Joe Fernandez
179.	67
180.	The French Open

DAVIS CUP HOSTS IN THE 1980s

181.	Prague	1980
182.	Stuttgart	1989
183.	Gothenburg	1987
184.	Melbourne	1986
185.	Grenoble	1982
186.	Gothenburg	1988
187.	Cincinnati	1981
188.	Melbourne	1983
189.	Munich	1985
190.	Gothenburg	1984

MEN'S SINGLES CHAMPION - 2

191.	Stefan Edberg	1990
192.	Rod Laver	1968
193.	Boris Becker	1985
194.	John McEnroe	1983
195.	Arthur Ashe	1975
196.	Pete Sampras	1998
197.	Andre Agassi	1992
198.	Jimmy Connors	1982
199.	Bjorn Borg	1977
200.	Stan Smith	1972

LADIES' SINGLES CHAMPION - 2

201.	Venus Williams	2000
202.	Jana Novotna	1998
203.	Evonne Cawley	1980
204.	Martina Hingis	1997
205.	Steffi Graf	1989
206.	Martina Navratilova	1985
207.	Ann Jones	1969
208.	Chris Evert Lloyd	1981
209.	Lindsay Davenport	1999
210.	Billie Jean King	1975

PAST MASTER - LEW HOAD

211. Australian
212. 2
213. Alan
214. 1957
215. Back problems
216. Ken Rosewall
217. The US Open
218. 1956
219. 4
220. The French Open (Singles 1956, Doubles 1953 & Mixed Doubles 1954)

WIMBLEDON - 1978

221. Bjorn Borg
222. Jimmy Connors
223. Tom Okker
224. Vitas Gerulaitis
225. Martina Navratilova
226. Chris Evert
227. Virginia Wade
228. R A J Hewitt & F D McMillan
229. Mrs G E Reid & Miss W M Turnbull
230. Betty Stove

THE NEARLY WOMEN

231.	Justine Henin-Hardenne	2001
232.	Venus Williams	2003
233.	Chris Evert Lloyd	1984
234.	Jana Novotna	1997
235.	Arantxa Sanchez-Vicario	1995
236.	Betty Stove	1977
237.	Nathalie Tauziat	1998
238.	Hana Mandlikova	1981
239.	Steffi Graf	1999
240.	Martina Navratilova	1988

PAST MASTER - JAN KODES

241. Czechoslovakian
242. John Newcombe
243. 1
244. 1973
245. 5th (1971)
246. Ilie Nastase

247. 2
248. Stan Smith
249. Czechoslovakian Championship
250. The Davis Cup (with Czechoslovakia)

LEGEND - MARIA BUENO

251. Brazilian
252. Esther
253. 3
254. 1959
255. 5
256. 1959, 1960, 1964 & 1966
257. The US Open (1966)
258. Doubles (1958)
259. The US Amateur Final
260. 4

WIMBLEDON - 1979

261. Bjorn Borg
262. Roscoe Tanner
263. Jimmy Connors
264. Pat Dupre
265. Martina Navratilova
266. Chris Evert Lloyd
267. Evonne Cawley
268. Peter Fleming & John McEnroe (USA)
269. Billie Jean King & Martina Navratilova
270. R A J Hewitt & Miss G R Stevens (RSA)

WIMBLEDON - 1980

271. Bjorn Borg
272. John McEnroe
273. Brian Gottfried
274. Jimmy Connors
275. Evonne Cawley
276. Chris Evert Lloyd
277. Tracey Austin
278. Peter McNamara & Paul McNamee
279. Miss K Jordan & Miss A E Smith
280. J R Austin & Miss T A Austin (USA)

THE FRENCH OPEN

281. Paris

282. Roland Garros
283. 1928
284. He was a pilot
285. 1891
286. Mary Pierce
287. 2000
288. 2
289. Kids Day
290. 3

THE AUSTRALIAN OPEN

291. January
292. 1905
293. The Australasian Championships
294. 1969
295. Melbourne
296. New Zealand
297. Ken Rosewall (18 & 37)
298. Martina Hingis
299. Roger Federer
300. Justine Henin-Hardenne

THE GRAND SLAM

301. Australian Open, French Open, US Open & Wimbledon
302. The French Open
303. Maureen Connolly
304. Rod Laver (1962 & 1969)
305. Donald Budge
306. The French Open
307. Wimbledon (by 4 years over the US Open)
308. Decoturf
309. Steffi Graf
310. Margaret Smith Court

WIMBLEDON - 1981

311. John McEnroe
312. Bjorn Borg
313. Rod Frawley
314. Jimmy Connors
315. Chris Evert Lloyd
316. Hana Mandlikova
317. Martina Navratilova
318. Peter Fleming & John McEnroe

319. Miss M Navratilova (USA) & Miss PH Shriver (USA)
320. Frew McMillan (RSA) & Betty Stove (NED)

MEN'S FRENCH OPEN CHAMPIONS - 1

321.	Jim Courier	1992
322.	Juan Carlos Ferrero	2003
323.	Ivan Lendl	1984
324.	Yevgeny Kafelnikov	1996
325.	Albert Costa	2002
326.	Michael Chang	1989
327.	Andre Agassi	1999
328.	Gaston Gaudio	2004
329.	Gustavo Kuerten	2000
330.	Bjorn Borg	1981

DAVIS CUP FINAL - 2004

331. Spain
332. USA
333. Spain
334. Spain 3, USA 2
335. Carlos Moya
336. Andy Roddick
337. Seville (Estadio Olimpico De Sevilla)
338. Juan Carlos Ferrero, Carlos Moya, Rafael Nadal & Tommy Robredo
339. Bob Bryan, Mike Brayn, Mardy Fish & Andy Roddick
340. Patrick McEnroe

2004 WINNERS

341.	Roger Federer	Wimbledon
342.	Justine Henin-Hardenne	Australian Open
343.	Roger Federer	Australian Open
344.	Anastasia Myskina	French Open
345.	Roger Federer	US Open
346.	Maria Sharapova	Wimbledon
347.	Gaston Gaudio	French Open
348.	Svetlana Kuznetsova	US Open
349.	Roger Federer	Masters
350.	Maria Sharapova	Masters

LADIES' FRENCH OPEN CHAMPIONS - 1

351.	Monica Seles	1990
352.	Arantxa Sanchez-Vicario	1994
353.	Steffi Graf	1996

354.	Chris Evert	1974
355.	Sue Barker	1976
356.	Martina Navratilova	1984
357.	Jennifer Capriati	2001
358.	Mary Pierce	2000
359.	Billie Jean King	1972
360.	Margaret Smith Court	1969

PAST MASTER - BORIS BECKER - 1

361. 1985
362. 17
363. 3
364. 1986 & 1989
365. 4
366. 1988, 1990, 1991 & 1995
367. Kevin Curren
368. Stefan Edberg (1988 & 1990)
369. Michael Stich (1991)
370. Pete Sampras (1995)

WORLD TEAM CUP - 2004

371. Chile
372. Australia
373. Red
374. Blue
375. Fernando Gonzalez & Nicolas Massu
376. Lleyton Hewitt & Mark Philippoussis
377. Germany
378. Argentina
379. Chile 2, Australia 1
380. ARAG

DELTA TOUR OF CHAMPIONS - 2000

381. John McEnroe
382. Henri Leconte
383. Bjorn Borg
384. Mats Wilander
385. Jimmy Connors
386. Mikael Pernfors
387. Pat Cash
388. Guy Forget
389. John McEnroe
390. Pat Cash

2004 CHAMPIONS TOUR RANKINGS

391.	Mats Wilander	5th
392.	Jim Courier	1st
393.	Pat Cash	10th
394.	John McEnroe	15th
395.	Boris Becker	6th
396.	Felip Dewulf	Joint 20th
397.	Sergi Bruguera	3rd
398.	Guy Forget	7th
399.	Jim Siemerink	Joint 16th
400.	Mikael Pernfors	14th

MEN'S US OPEN CHAMPIONS - 2

401.	Patrick Rafter	1998
402.	Pete Sampras	1996
403.	Andre Agassi	1999
404.	Mats Wilander	1988
405.	Boris Becker	1989
406.	Guillermo Vilas	1977
407.	Jimmy Connors	1983
408.	Stefan Edberg	1991
409.	John McEnroe	1980
410.	Ivan Lendl	1987

LADIES' US OPEN CHAMPIONS - 2

411.	Billie Jean King	1974
412.	Venus Williams	2001
413.	Lindsay Davenport	1998
414.	Margaret Smith Court	1973
415.	Arantxa Sanchez-Vicario	1994
416.	Serena Williams	1999
417.	Steffi Graf	1996
418.	Chris Evert	1975
419.	Monica Seles	1991
420.	Martina Navratilova	1983

THE 2000 OLYMPIC GAMES

421. Yevgeny Kafelnikov (Russia)
422. Tommy Haas (Germany)
423. Venus Williams (USA)
424. Elena Dementieva (Russia)
425. Mark Woodforde and Todd Woodbridge
426. Roger Federer (2003 & 2004 Wimbledon Champion)

427. Monica Seles (USA)
428. Jelena Dokic (Australia)
429. 64
430. Australia (Sydney)

MEN'S FRENCH OPEN CHAMPIONS - 2

431.	Jim Courier	1991
432.	Carlos Moya	1998
433.	Ivan Lendl	1987
434.	Thomas Muster	1995
435.	Mats Wilander	1988
436.	Sergi Bruguera	1993
437.	Andres Gomez	1990
438.	Jan Kodes	1971
439.	Gustavo Kuerten	2001
440.	Bjorn Borg	1976

LADIES' FRENCH OPEN CHAMPIONS - 2

441.	Mima Jausovec	1977
442.	Chris Evert Lloyd	1980
443.	Serena Williams	2002
444.	Hana Mandlikova	1981
445.	Martina Navratilova	1982
446.	Arantxa Sanchez-Vicario	1989
447.	Steffi Graf	1999
448.	Monica Seles	1992
449.	Iva Majoli	1997
450.	Chris Evert	1975

PAST MASTER - BORIS BECKER - 2

451. 7
452. Michael Chang (17 years & 3 months)
453. 1994 & 1996
454. The Masters
455. 1989
456. 2
457. 1991 & 1996
458. Barcelona (1992)
459. Germany's Davis Cup Team
460. 6th (September 1986)

WORLD TEAM CUP - 2003

461. Chile

462. Czech Republic
463. Blue
464. Red
465. Fernando Gonzalez & Marcelo Rios
466. Jiri Novak & Radel Stepanek
467. Argentina
468. Australia, Spain & USA all finished with a 1-2 record
469. Chile 2, Czech Republic 1
470. Germany (Dusseldorf)

SERENA WILLIAMS

471. 2 (2002 & 2003)
472. Her sister Venus (and in 2003)
473. The Australian Open
474. 1999
475. Amelie Mauresmo
476. The US Open (1999)
477. Jennifer Capriati
478. The French Open (2002)
479. Justine Henin-Hardenne
480. 14 (although the WTA did not recognise entrants of that age)

WTA SANEX CHAMPIONSHIPS - 2001

481. Serena
482. Lindsay Davenport
483. Kim Clijsters & Sandrine Testud
484. Jennifer Capriati
485. Jelena Dokic
486. Munich
487. $750,000
488. Arantxa Sanchez-Vicario
489. Justine Henin-Hardenne
490. 7th

WTA HOME DEPOT CHAMPIONSHIPS 2002

491. Kim Clijsters
492. Serena Williams
493. Jennifer Capriati & Venus Williams
494. Porsche
495. Justine Henin-Hardenne
496. Daniela Hantuchova
497. Los Angeles
498. $765,000

499. Elena Dementieva
500. Lindsay Davenport

THE BOYS' SINGLES FINAL AT WIMBLEDON

501. Roger Federer (Boys' Singles Champion 1998 & Men's Singles Champion 2003)
502. Danish (K Nielsen)
503. Mark Philippoussis
504. Pat Cash (Wimbledon Champion 1987)
505. Stefan Edberg (1988 & 1990)
506. Bjorn Borg
507. Chris Lewis
508. Ivan Lendl
509. Never
510. Roger Federer (Boys' Singles Champion 1998 & Men's Singles Champion 2003 & 2004)

WIMBLEDON BOYS' SINGLES CHAMPIONS

511.	F Mergea (ROM)	2003
512.	N Mahut (FRA)	2000
513.	W Whitehouse (RSA)	1997
514.	J Melzer (AUT)	1999
515.	V Voltchkov (BLR)	1996
516.	S Humphries (USA)	1994
517.	T Reid (AUS)	2002
518.	G Monfils (FRA)	2004
519.	R Valent (SUI)	2001
520.	O Mutis (FRA)	1995

PAST MASTER - ARTHUR ASHE

521. Robert
522. Lieutenant
523. The US Open
524. 1975
525. Jimmy Connors
526. The Australian Open
527. 11
528. 10
529. 6th
530. French (1971) & Australian (1977)

PAST MASTER - JAROSLAV DROBNY

531. Czechoslovakia

532.	Egyptian
533.	Left handed
534.	1954 (to his death in 2001)
535.	Ice-Hockey
536.	1 (1954)
537.	The French Open Men's Singles
538.	The French Open (1948)
539.	1948 (Ice Hockey with Czechoslovakia)
540.	Ken Rosewall

WIMBLEDON RECORDS

541.	USA
542.	USA
543.	Pete Sampras
544.	Willie Renshaw
545.	Miss Elizabeth M Ryan
546.	4
547.	7
548.	Australia
549.	Boris Becker (aged 17 in 1985)
550.	Rod Laver (in 1959)

LADIES' DOUBLES WINNERS

551.	Mrs L W King & Miss M Navratilova	1979
552.	Miss M Navratilova & Miss P Shriver	1983
553.	Miss K Clijsters & Miss A Sugiyama	2003
554.	Miss M Hingis & Miss J Novotna	1998
555.	Miss B C Fernandez & Miss N M Zvereva	1993
556.	Miss V E Williams & Miss S J Williams	2002
557.	Miss K Jordan & Miss P D Smylie	1985
558.	Miss J Novotna & Miss H Sukova	1989
559.	Mrs R L Cawley & Miss J C Russell	1977
560.	Miss C M Evert & Miss M Navratilova	1976

VIRGINIA SLIMS CHAMPIONSHIP WINNERS

561.	Chris Evert	1972
562.	Martina Navratilova	1985
563.	Rosie Casals	1976
564.	Evonne Goolagong	1974
565.	Virginia Wade	1975
566.	Wendy Turnbull	1978
567.	Martina Navratilova	1983
568.	Martina Navratilova	1977

569.	Chris Evert	1973
570.	Martina Navratilova	1984

LADIES' DOUBLES AT WIMBLEDON

571. 2
572. 2003
573. 1985 (Mrs P D Smylie with Miss K Jordan)
574. Gabriela Sabatini
575. Miss C Black & Miss R Stubbs
576. Miss L I Savchenko & Miss N M Zvereva
577. Helena Sukova
578. Lindsay Davenport
579. Arantxa Sanchez-Vicario
580. Miss C G Kohde-Kilsh (GER) & Miss H Sukova (TCH)

2001 SANEX LADIES' DOUBLES CHAMPIONSHIPS

581. Lisa Raymond & Rennae Stubbs
582. Australia & USA
583. Cara Black & Elena Likhovtseva
584. Zimbabwe
585. Munich
586. $300,000
587. $3,000,000
588. Virginia Ruano Pascual & Paola Suarez
589. Kimberly Po-Messerli & Nathalie Tauziat
590. Decoturf

MEN'S MULTIPLE CHAMPION

591.	Don Budge	2
592.	John Newcombe	3
593.	Bjorn Borg	5
594.	Rod Laver	4
595.	Pete Sampras	7
596.	John McEnroe	3
597.	Jimmy Connors	2
598.	Fred Perry	3
599.	Boris Becker	3
600.	Laurie Doherty	5

MEN'S DOUBLES CHAMPIONS

601.	2002	T Woodbridge (AUS) & J Bjorkman (SWE)
602.	1986	J Nystrom & M Wilander (SWE)
603.	2001	D Johnson & J Palmer (USA)

604.	1998	J Eltingh & P Haarhuis (NED)
605.	1999	M Bhupathi & L Paes (IND)
606.	1978	R Hewitt & F McMillan (SA)
607.	1996	T Woodbridge & M Woodforde (AUS)
608.	1983	P Fleming & J McEnroe (USA)
609.	1992	J McEnroe (USA) & M Stich (GER)
610.	1974	J Newcombe & A Roche (AUS)

LADIES' MULTIPLE CHAMPION

611.	Evonne Goolagong Cawley	2
612.	Louise Brough	4
613.	Martina Navratilova	9
614.	Steffi Graf	7
615.	Margaret Smith Court	3
616.	Billie Jean King	6
617.	Helen Willis Moody	8
618.	Chris Evert Lloyd	3
619.	Maureen Connolly	3
620.	Suzanne Lenglen	6

LEGEND - EVONNE GOOLAGONG CAWLEY

621.	Australian
622.	Fay
623.	2
624.	1971 & 1980
625.	3
626.	1972, 1975 & 1976
627.	Margaret Court & Chris Evert Lloyd
628.	Billie Jean King (1972 & 1975)
629.	4
630.	1974, 1975, 1976 & 1977

THE NEARLY MEN

631.	Patrick Rafter	2001
632.	Boris Becker	1995
633.	David Nalbandian	2002
634.	Ivan Lendl	1987
635.	Goran Ivanisevic	1998
636.	Jimmy Connors	1975
637.	Stefan Edberg	1989
638.	Kevin Curren	1985
639.	Jim Courier	1993
640.	Cedric Pioline	1997

MEN'S US OPEN CHAMPIONS - 1

641.	Patrick Rafter	1997
642.	Pete Sampras	2002
643.	Andre Agassi	1994
644.	Ilie Nastase	1972
645.	Marat Safin	2000
646.	Arthur Ashe	1968
647.	Jimmy Connors	1978
648.	Lleyton Hewitt	2001
649.	John McEnroe	1984
650.	Ivan Lendl	1986

LADIES' US OPEN CHAMPIONS - 1

651.	Martina Hingis	1997
652.	Venus Williams	2000
653.	Tracey Austin	1979
654.	Hana Mandlikova	1985
655.	Gabriela Sabatini	1990
656.	Serena Williams	2002
657.	Steffi Graf	1993
658.	Chris Evert	1977
659.	Monica Seles	1992
660.	Martina Navratilova	1987

THE 2004 OLYMPIC GAMES

661. Nicolas Massu
662. Mardy Fish
663. Justine Henin-Hardenne
664. Amelie Mauresmo
665. Andy Roddick
666. Czechoslovakian (Czech Republic)
667. Taylor Dent (USA) & Fernando Gonzalez (Chile)
668. Alicia Molik & Anastasia Myskina
669. Martina Navratilova
670. Nicolas Massu (Men's Singles & Men's Doubles)

WIMBLEDON - 1982

671. Jimmy Connors
672. John McEnroe
673. Mark Edmondson
674. Tim Mayotte
675. Martina Navratilova
676. Chris Evert Lloyd

677. Billie Jean KIng
678. Peter McNamara & Paul McNamee
679. Martina Navratilova (USA) & Pam Shriver (USA)
680. Kevin Curren

PAST MASTER - STEFAN EDBERG

681. 6
682. 2
683. Boris Becker (1988 & 1990)
684. The French Open
685. Ivan Lendl
686. 8 (1985-1994)
687. ATP Player of the Year
688. 1984 (Los Angeles when tennis was a demonstration sport)
689. 4
690. 41

WIMBLEDON - 1983

691. John McEnroe
692. Chris Lewis
693. Ivan Lendl
694. Kevin Curren
695. Martina Navratilova
696. Andrea Jaeger
697. Billie Jean King
698. Peter Fleming & John McEnroe
699. Martina Navratilova & Pam Shriver
700. John Lloyd

LEGEND - VIRGINIA WADE

701. 1977
702. Betty Stove
703. Ginny
704. Queen Elizabeth II (it was the Jubilee Final)
705. 31
706. 3
707. The French Open
708. The US Open
709. Billie Jean King
710. 55

WIMBLEDON - 1984

711. John McEnroe

712. Jimmy Connors
713. Pat Cash
714. Ivan Lendl
715. Martina Navratilova
716. Chris Evert Lloyd
717. Billie Jean King
718. Peter Fleming & John McEnroe
719. Martina Navratilova & Pam Shriver
720. John Lloyd & Wendy Turnbull

PAST MASTER - TONY ROCHE

721. Australian
722. The French Open (1966)
723. 2nd
724. 1969
725. 5
726. John Newcombe
727. 14
728. 12
729. Australia's Davis Cup Team
730. The Italian

WIMBLEDON - 1985

731. Boris Becker
732. Kevin Curren
733. Jimmy Connors
734. Heinz Guenthardt
735. Martina Navratilova
736. Chris Evert Lloyd
737. Zina Garrison
738. H P Guenthardt (SUI) & B Taroczy (HUN)
739. Miss K Jordan (USA) & Mrs P D Smylie (AUS)
740. Paul McNamee (AUS) & Martina Navratilova (USA)

LEGEND - STEFFI GRAF

741. 107
742. 22
743. Wimbledon (7)
744. The French Open (1987)
745. 9
746. 1988
747. 1985
748. The Federation Cup

749. 30

750. Martina Navratilova (1987)

WIMBLEDON - 1986

751. Boris Becker
752. Ivan Lendl
753. Henri Leconte
754. Slobodan Zivojinovic
755. Martina Navratilova
756. Hana Mandlikova
757. Gabriela Sabatini
758. J K Nystrom & M A O Wilander
759. Martina Navratilova & Pam Shriver
760. K E Flach & Miss K Jordan

PAST MASTER - JOHN McENROE

761. 1980
762. Bjorn Borg
763. Bjorn Borg
764. 7
765. The US Open
766. 1984
767. 3
768. Jimmy Connors
769. 1978
770. Germany (his father was stationed there with the US Air Force)

WIMBLEDON - 1987

771. Pat Cash
772. Ivan Lendl
773. Jimmy Connors
774. Stefan Edberg
775. Martina Navratilova
776. Steffi Graf
777. Chris Evert
778. K E Flach & R A Seguso
779. Miss C G Kohde-Kilsh (GER) & Miss H Sukova (TCH)
780. Jeremy Bates & Jo Durie

LEGEND - CHRIS EVERT

781. Margaret Court
782. Billie Jean King
783. 157

784. 1973
785. The French Open (1974)
786. 3
787. 1974, 1976 & 1981
788. John Lloyd
789. Olga Morozova
790. Evonne Cawley

WIMBLEDON - 1988

791. Stefan Edberg
792. Boris Becker
793. Ivan Lendl
794. Miloslav Mecir
795. Steffi Graf
796. Martina Navratilova
797. Chris Evert
798. KE Flach & RA Seguso
799. Steffi Graf (GER) & Gabriela Sabatini (ARG)
800. S E Stewart & Miss Z L Garrison

FACTS & TRIVIA - 1

801. 1975 (November)
802. Steffi Graf (Germany)
803. Arthur Ashe
804. Buster Mottram
805. Billie Jean King (age 39)
806. John McEnroe
807. Stefan Edberg
808. Ivan Lendl
809. Jean Rene Lacoste
810. The Australian Open

WIMBLEDON - 1989

811. Boris Becker
812. Stefan Edberg
813. John McEnroe
814. Ivan Lendl
815. Steffi Graf
816. Martina Navratilova
817. Chris Evert
818. J B Fitzgerald (AUS) & A Jarryd (SWE)
819. Jana Novotna & Helena Sukova
820. J R Pugh (USA) & Miss J Novotna (TCH)

CHAMPIONS - 1

821. Evonne Goolagong
822. The Men's Doubles Championship
823. John Newcombe
824. Arthur Ashe
825. Ellen Roosevelt
826. 1972
827. Chris Evert
828. John McEnroe
829. Yannick Noah
830. Kerry Melville (Australian), Helga Niessen (French), Billie Jean King (Wimbledon) & Rosie Casals (US Open)

WIMBLEDON - 1990

831. Stefan Edberg
832. Boris Becker
833. Ivan Lendl
834. Goran Ivanisevic
835. Martina Navratilova
836. Zina Garrison
837. Steffi Graf
838. R D Leach & J R Pugh
839. Jana Novotna & Helena Sukova
840. RD Leach & Miss Z L Garrison

PAST MASTER - ILIE NASTASE

841. Bucharest
842. 4
843. 1971, 1972, 1973 & 1975
844. Never
845. Stan Smith (1972)
846. Bjorn Borg
847. 57
848. 2
849. 1967 & 1973
850. Romania's Davis Cup Team

WIMBLEDON - 1991

851. Michael Stich
852. Boris Becker
853. Stefan Edberg
854. David Wheaton
855. Steffi Graf

856. Gabriela Sabatini (Argentina)
857. Mary Joe Fernandez (lost to Graf) & Jennifer Capriati (lost to Sabatini)
858. J B Fitzgerald (AUS) & A P Jarryd (SWE)
859. Miss L I Savchenko & Miss N M Zvereva
860. J B Fitzgerald & Mrs P D Smylie

WIMBLEDON - 1992

861. Andre Agassi
862. Goran Ivanisevic
863. John McEnroe
864. Pete Sampras
865. Steffi Graf
866. Monica Seles
867. Martina Navratilova
868. John McEnroe & Michael Stich
869. Miss B C Fernandez (USA) & Miss N M Zvereva (CIS)
870. C Suk (TCH) & Mrs A Neiland (LAT)

FACTS & TRIVIA - 2

871. The Sunshine Girl
872. Chris Evert
873. 268
874. Prague
875. John McEnroe
876. Stefan Edberg
877. Roy Emerson (Australian, French & US Open) & Marty Mulligan (Wimbledon)
878. Bjorn Borg (age 17)
879. Ivan Lendl (Czechoslovakia)
880. Jennifer Capriati (age 14)

WIMBLEDON - 1993

881. Pete Sampras
882. Jim Courier
883. Boris Becker
884. Stefan Edberg
885. Steffi Graf
886. Jana Novotna
887. Conchita Martinez
888. Todd Woodbridge & Mark Woodforde (AUS)
889. Miss B C Fernandez (USA) & Miss N M Zvereva (BLR)
890. Mark Woodforde (AUS) & Martina Navratilova (USA)

THE MEN'S GAME

891. R A "Pancho" Gonzalez (aged 41)
892. Heinz Guenthardt
893. Mark Woodforde
894. 1975
895. Andre Agassi
896. Bjorn Borg
897. Ilie Nastase
898. Arthur Ashe
899. The Italian
900. Ivan Lendl

THE LADIES' GAME

901. Chris Evert
902. Catarina Linqvist
903. Pam Shriver
904. Evonne Goolagong
905. Virginia Wade
906. Maria Bueno
907. Chris Evert (Australian), Natalia Zvereva (French), Martina Navratilova (Wimbledon) & Gabriela Sabatini (US Open)
908. The Olympic gold medal (she defeated Gabriela Sabatini in the Ladies' Singles Final - a "Golden Slam" for 1988)
909. The USA Wightman Cup Team
910. Billie Jean King beat Christine Truman 19-17

WIMBLEDON - 1994

911. Pete Sampras
912. Goran Ivanisevic
913. Todd Martin
914. Boris Becker
915. Conchita Martinez
916. Martina Navratilova
917. Gigi Fernandez (lost to Navratilova) & Lori McNeil (lost to Martinez)
918. Todd Woodbridge & Mark Woodforde (AUS)
919. Jana Novotna (CZE) & Arantxa Sanchez-Vicario (ESP)
920. Todd Woodbridge (AUS) and Helena Sukova (CZE)

MEN'S CHAMPIONS

921. Stefan Edberg (1988, 1989, 1990, 1992 & 1995)
922. Pete Sampras (286) & Ivan Lendl (270)
923. 160
924. Arthur Ashe

925. Patrick
926. Ilie Nastase
927. 7 (5 Czechoslovakian, 1 French & 1 Italian)
928. John McEnroe
929. The US Open
930. 1

LADIES CHAMPIONS

931. Chris Evert
932. 19
933. Margaret Court
934. Rosie Casals, Françoise Durr, Ann Haydon Jones & Billie Jean King
935. Steffi Graf
936. Virginia Wade (1967-1983)
937. Evonne Goolagong Cawley
938. Martina Navratilova
939. Steffi Graf
940. 4 (1981-1984)

WIMBLEDON - 1995

941. Pete Sampras
942. Boris Becker
943. Goran Ivanisevic
944. Andre Agassi
945. Steffi Graf
946. Arantxa Sanchez-Vicario
947. Jana Novotna
948. Todd Woodbridge & Mark Woodforde
949. Jana Novotna (CZE) & Arantxa Sanchez-Vicario (ESP)
950. Martina Navratilova

LEGEND - MARTINA NAVRATILOVA

951. 9
952. 1978, 1979, 1982-1987 & 1990
953. Chris Evert
954. Prague (Revnice)
955. Conchita Martinez
956. 20 (equalling Billie Jean King's record)
957. The Australian Open - 4 times
958. 16
959. Pam Shriver
960. 1978

FIRST SET

961. Martina Navratilova (after her defection to the USA)
962. Arthur Ashe
963. Wimbledon
964. Ilie Nastase
965. Maria Bueno (her previous 62 victories were won when she was an Amateur)
966. Raul Ramirez
967. Chris Evert
968. John & Patrick McEnroe (John won by 2 sets to 1)
969. Evonne Goolagong Cawley
970. Ivan Lendl

WIMBLEDON - 1996

971. Richard Krajicek
972. Malivai Washington
973. Jason Stoltenberg
974. Todd Martin
975. Steffi Graf
976. Arantxa Sanchez-Vicario
977. Martina Hingis
978. Todd Woodbridge & Mark Woodforde
979. Martina Hingis (SUI) & Helena Sukova (CZE)
980. C Suk & Miss H Sukova (CZE)

SECOND SET

981. 9 (1982-1990)
982. Martina Hingis (aged 15 - 1996 Doubles with Helena Sukova)
983. Tennis Coach
984. John McEnroe
985. 27
986. Guillermo Vilas
987. Virginia Wade
988. Ilie Nastase
989. Martina Navratilova
990. Boris Becker

WIMBLEDON - 1997

991. Pete Sampras
992. Cedric Pioline
993. Todd Woodbridge
994. Michael Stich
995. Martina Hingis
996. Jana Novotna

997. Anna Kournikova
998. Todd Woodbridge & Mark Woodforde
999. Miss B C Fernandez (USA) & Miss N M Zvereva (BLR)
1000. C Suk & Miss H Sukova (CZE)

PAST MASTER - PETE SAMPRAS

1001. The US Open
1002. 1990
1003. Andre Agassi
1004. 7
1005. 1993-1995 & 1997-2000
1006. Patrick Rafter
1007. 14
1008. The US Open (2002) defeating Andre Agassi
1009. 1990, 1993, 1995, 1996 & 2002
1010. The French Open

THE EARLY 1970s AT WIMBLEDON

1011. John Newcombe (1970)
1012. Margaret Court (1970)
1013. Evonne Goolagong
1014. Stan Smith
1015. John Newcombe & Tony Roche
1016. Billie Jean King (1973 & 1974)
1017. Ken Rosewall
1018. Rosie Casals (USA) & Ilie Nastase (Romania)
1019. John Newcombe (1970 & 1971)
1020. Rosie Casals & Billie Jean King

WIMBLEDON - 1998

1021. Pete Sampras
1022. Goran Ivanisevic
1023. Tim Henman
1024. Richard Krajicek
1025. Jana Novotna
1026. Nathalie Tauziat
1027. Martina Hingis
1028. J F Eltingh & P V N Haarhuis
1029. They were the last 2 Ladies' Singles Winners - Martina Hingis (1997) & Jana Novotna (1998)
1030. M N Mirnyi (BLR) & Miss S J Williams (USA)

THIRD SET

1031. Steffi Graf
1032. Pete Sampras (2000)
1033. 9
1034. The US Open
1035. Martina Navratilova
1036. Ivan Lendl
1037. Lindsay Davenport
1038. Arthur Ashe
1039. Chris Evert
1040. John McEnroe

WIMBLEDON IN THE 1960s

1041. Rod Laver
1042. John Newcombe & Tony Roche
1043. Billie Jean King
1044. Maria Bueno
1045. Fred Stolle
1046. Angela Mortimer beat Christine Truman by 2 sets to 1
1047. Rod Laver
1048. Maria Bueno
1049. Manuel Santana
1050. Ann Jones

MEN'S GRAND SLAM SINGLES WINNERS

1051.	Jimmy Connors	8
1052.	Roy Emerson	12
1053.	Boris Becker	6
1054.	Bjorn Borg	11
1055.	Jim Courier	4
1056.	Ivan Lendl	8
1057.	Rod Laver	11
1058.	Pete Sampras	14
1059.	Andre Agassi	8
1060.	John McEnroe	7

LADIES' GRAND SLAM SINGLES WINNERS

1061.	Chris Evert Lloyd	18
1062.	Martina Navratilova	18
1063.	Martina Hingis	5
1064.	Billie Jean King	10
1065.	Maureen Connolly	9
1066.	Steffi Graf	22

1067.	Margaret Smith Court	24
1068.	Maria Bueno	7
1069.	Monica Seles	9
1070.	Helen Willis Moody	19

PAST MASTER - FRED PERRY

1071. Stockport
1072. John
1073. 3
1074. 1934, 1935 & 1936
1075. 1 (1934)
1076. The French Open (1934)
1077. 3
1078. 1933, 1934 & 1936
1079. Table tennis
1080. The production of tennis clothes

ANDRE AGASSI

1081. Las Vegas
1082. 1986
1083. Boxing
1084. Atlanta in 1996
1085. Wimbledon
1086. 1992
1087. Boris Becker (Quarter-Finals) & John McEnroe (Semi-Finals)
1088. 1995
1089. The Nick Bollettieri Tennis Academy in Bradenton, Florida, USA
1090. The Australian Open - 4 times (1995, 2000, 2001 & 2003)

WIMBLEDON - 1999

1091. Pete Sampras
1092. Andre Agassi
1093. Tim Henman (to Pete Sampras)
1094. Patrick Rafter
1095. Lindsay Davenport
1096. Steffi Graf
1097. Mirjana Lucic & Alexandra Stevenson
1098. M S Bhupathi & L A Paes
1099. Miss L A Davenport & Miss C M Morariu
1100. L A Paes (IND) & Miss L M Raymond (USA)

FOURTH SET

1101. Evonne Cawley beat Chris Evert 6-1, 7-6 (7-1)

1102. Andres Gimeno (Australian), Ken Rosewall (French), John Newcombe (Wimbledon) & Tony Roche (US Open)
1103. Chris Evert
1104. 7
1105. Martina Navratilova (312 between 1973-2003)
1106. Ivan Lendl
1107. The Italian Open (Singles)
1108. Ilie Nastase
1109. Steffi Graf
1110. Arthur Ashe

WIMBLEDON - 2000

1111. Pete Sampras
1112. Patrick Rafter
1113. Vladimir Voltchkov
1114. Andre Agassi
1115. Venus Williams
1116. Lindsay Davenport
1117. Serena Williams
1118. Todd Woodbridge & Mark Woodforde
1119. Serena & Venus Williams
1120. Lleyton Hewitt (AUS) & Kim Clijsters (BEL)

FACTS & TRIVIA - 3

1121. Steffi Graf
1122. 2 (1988 & 1989)
1123. Evonne Goolagong
1124. 35
1125. Boris Becker
1126. Chris Evert
1127. Stefan Edberg
1128. Martina Navratilova
1129. Pete Sampras
1130. Jimmy Connors

WIMBLEDON - 2001

1131. Goran Ivanisevic
1132. Patrick Rafter
1133. Tim Henman
1134. Andre Agassi
1135. Venus Williams
1136. Justine Henin-Hardenne
1137. Lindsay Davenport

1138. D J Johnson & J E Palmer
1139. Miss K Clijsters (BEL) & Miss A Sugiyama (JPN)
1140. L Friedl (CZE) & Miss D Hantuchova (SVK)

PAST MASTER - MATS WILANDER

1141. Ivan Lendl
1142. Wimbledon
1143. The French Open
1144. 1982 (aged 17, the youngest ever French Open Champion at the time)
1145. 8
1146. John McEnroe
1147. 1983 (December), 1984 (December) & 1988
1148. The ATP Tour Player of the Year Award
1149. No. 1 (in 1988)
1150. Marat Safin

WIMBLEDON - 2002

1151. Lleyton Hewitt
1152. David Nalbandian
1153. Lleyton Hewitt (in the Semi-Finals)
1154. Xavier Malisse
1155. Serena Williams
1156. Venus Williams
1157. Amelie Mauresmo
1158. Jonas Bjorkman (SWE) & Todd Woodbridge (AUS)
1159. Serena & Venus Williams
1160. M Bhupathi (IND) & Miss E Likhovteva (RUS)

DEUCE

1161. Martina Navratilova & Pam Shriver
1162. Boris Becker
1163. Maureen Connolly
1164. Sarah
1165. Chris Evert
1166. Evonne Goolagong
1167. Maria Bueno
1168. Mats Wilander
1169. Martina Navratilova
1170. Sydney (Glebe)

ADVANTAGE

1171. Arthur Ashe
1172. Chris Evert

1173. Fireman
1174. Chris Evert Lloyd
1175. Jimmy Connors
1176. Neale Fisher
1177. 15
1178. 43
1179. Martina Navratilova
1180. Fred Stolle

TIM HENMAN

1181. Oxford
1182. The bone disease - Osteochondritis Dissecans
1183. National Junior Championship
1184. 1993
1185. Top 30
1186. The ATP Most Improved Player Award
1187. Australia (in Sydney in 1997)
1188. The BBC's Sports Personality of the Year Award
1189. Greg Rusedski (6th September - Greg in 1973 & Tim in 1974)
1190. 4 (1998, 1999, 2001 & 2002)

GAME, SET & MATCH

1191. Bjorn Borg
1192. Chris Evert
1193. Gustavo Kuerten
1194. Steffi Graf
1195. Boris Becker
1196. Evonne Cawley (1973-1976, she never won it)
1197. S J Matthews
1198. 2nd (1968)
1199. Arthur Ashe
1200. 14 (10 Ladies' Doubles & 4 Mixed Doubles)

FOR THE EXPERT

EXPERT - PAST MASTER - JIMMY CONNORS

1201. 54
1202. Belleville, Illinois
1203. 1972
1204. Israel (1989)
1205. Australian Open, US Open & Wimbledon
1206. 3

1207. 1976, 1981 & 1984
1208. Intercollegiate
1209. Stan Smith
1210. 16

EXPERT - MEN'S SINGLES CHAMPION

1211.	Lew Hoad	1956
1212.	Roy Emerson	1964
1213.	Rod Laver	1962
1214.	Neale Fisher	1960
1215.	Frank Sedgman	1952
1216.	Jaroslav Drobny	1954
1217.	Ashley Cooper	1958
1218.	Chuck McKinley	1963
1219.	Alex Olmedo	1959
1220.	Manuel Santana	1966

EXPERT - LADIES' SINGLES CHAMPION

1221.	Maria Bueno	1964
1222.	Karen Hantze (Susman)	1962
1223.	Louise Brough	1955
1224.	Billie Jean King	1966
1225.	Angela Mortimer	1961
1226.	Margaret Smith	1965
1227.	Althea Gibson	1958
1228.	Shirley Fry	1956
1229.	Maureen Connolly	1953
1230.	Doris Hart	1951

EXPERT - WIMBLEDON - 2004

1231. Conchita Martinez
1232. 5
1233. 13
1234. Lleyton Hewitt (the 2002 Champion)
1235. Mary Pierce
1236. Mario Ancic (Semi-Finals)
1237. K Sprem (Quarter-Finals)
1238. Ai Sugiyama
1239. Lindsay Davenport (the 1999 Champion in the Semi-Finals)
1240. Sjeng Schalken

EXPERT - BJORN BORG

1241. 1956

1242. Rune
1243. Sodertaljie
1244. Mats Wilander
1245. The Davis Cup (with Sweden, their first victory)
1246. John McEnroe
1247. 6
1248. 1981 (French Open)
1249. Rod Laver
1250. Vitas Gerulaitis

EXPERT - MEN'S DOUBLES CHAMPIONS

1251.	1977	R Case & G Masters (AUS)
1252.	1976	B Gottfried (USA) & R Ramirez (MEX)
1253.	1975	V Gerulaitis & A Mayer (USA)
1254.	1982	P McNamara & P McNamee (AUS)
1255.	1979	P Fleming & J McEnroe (USA)
1256.	1985	H Gunthardt (SWI) & B Taroczy (HUN)
1257.	1973	J Connors (USA) & I Nastase (ROM)
1258.	1972	R Hewitt & F McMillan (SA)
1259.	1971	R Emerson & R Laver (AUS)
1260.	1970	J Newcombe & A Roche (AUS)

EXPERT - MEN'S ATP FINAL RANKINGS FOR 2004

1261.	S Grosjean	15
1262.	G Canas	11
1263.	N Kiefer	20
1264.	M Youzhny	16
1265.	D Hrbaty	14
1266.	J Johansson	12
1267.	T Robredo	13
1268.	V Spadea	19
1269.	T Haas	17
1270.	N Massu	18

EXPERT - LADIES' WTP FINAL RANKINGS FOR 2004

1271.	S F'ina-Elia	10
1272.	A Sugiyama	17
1273.	N Petrova	12
1274.	A Molik	13
1275.	F Schiavone	19
1276.	P Suarez	16
1277.	V Zvonareva	11
1278.	E Bovina	15

1279.	K Sprem	18
1280.	P Schnyder	14

EXPERT - IVAN LENDL

1281. 3
1282. 1985, 1986 & 1987
1283. Jimmy Connors (1974) & Guillermo Vilas (1977) (Ivan Lendl - 1982)
1284. Ostrava
1285. 1992
1286. 8
1287. 19
1288. 8 (1982-1989)
1289. 23
1290. The Davis Cup (with Czechoslovakia)

EXPERT - MEN'S ATP FINAL RANKINGS FOR 1997

1291.	Albert Costa	19
1292.	Goran Ivanisevic	15
1293.	Tim Henman	17
1294.	Richard Krajicek	11
1295.	Felix Mantilla	16
1296.	Alex Corretja	12
1297.	Mark Philippoussis	18
1298.	Petr Korda	13
1299.	Gustavo Kuerten	14
1300.	Cedric Pioline	20

EXPERT - LEGEND - BILLIE JEAN KING

1301. 37
1302. The Italian Championship
1303. The Wightman Cup (with Team USA)
1304. 2
1305. 1995 & 1996
1306. The Australian Open
1307. 1966
1308. Evonne Cawley
1309. 1967 & 1973
1310. 38

EXPERT - THE NEARLY MEN

1311.	Jimmy Connors	1978
1312.	Ken Rosewall	1974
1313.	Roscoe Tanner	1979

1314.	Ilie Nastase	1976
1315.	John Newcombe	1969
1316.	Boris Becker	1990
1317.	Bjorn Borg	1981
1318.	Stan Smith	1971
1319.	Ivan Lendl	1986
1320.	Chris Lewis	1983

EXPERT - THE NEARLY WOMEN

1321.	Arantxa Sanchez-Vicario	1996
1322.	Lindsay Davenport	2000
1323.	Martina Navratilova	1994
1324.	Evonne Cawley	1976
1325.	Gabriela Sabatini	1991
1326.	Chris Evert	1978
1327.	Monica Seles	1992
1328.	Steffi Graf	1987
1329.	Andrea Jaeger	1983
1330.	Zina Garrison	1990

EXPERT - MEN'S US OPEN CHAMPIONS

1331.	John Newcombe	1973
1332.	Jimmy Connors	1976
1333.	Rod Laver	1969
1334.	Fred Stolle	1966
1335.	John McEnroe	1979
1336.	Roy Emerson	1964
1337.	Stan Smith	1971
1338.	Manuel Orantes	1975
1339.	Manuel Santana	1965
1340.	Ken Rosewall	1970

EXPERT - LADIES' US OPEN CHAMPIONS

1341.	Martina Navratilova	1986
1342.	Chris Evert Lloyd	1980
1343.	Darlene Hard	1961
1344.	Shirley Fry	1956
1345.	Margaret Smith Court	1970
1346.	Virginia Wade	1968
1347.	Althea Gibson	1958
1348.	Billie Jean King	1967
1349.	Maria Bueno	1963
1350.	Steffi Graf	1988

EXPERT - THE AUSTRALIAN OPEN

1351.	Norman Brookes Challenge Cup
1352.	1972
1353.	Rebound Ace
1354.	Daphne Akhurst Memorial Cup
1355.	Rod Laver
1356.	3
1357.	Margaret Smith Court
1358.	11
1359.	Martina Navratilova
1360.	Mats Wilander

EXPERT - MEN'S FRENCH OPEN CHAMPIONS

1361.	Bjorn Borg	1975
1362.	Ilie Nastase	1973
1363.	Guillermo Vilas	1977
1364.	Andres Gimeno	1972
1365.	Ken Rosewall	1968
1366.	Mats Wilander	1982
1367.	Adriano Panatta	1976
1368.	Roy Emerson	1963
1369.	Tony Roche	1966
1370.	Rod Laver	1962

EXPERT - LADIES' FRENCH OPEN CHAMPIONS

1371.	Steffi Graf	1993
1372.	Arantxa Sanchez-Vicario	1998
1373.	Chris Evert Lloyd	1986
1374.	Virginia Ruzici	1978
1375.	Evonne Goolagong	1971
1376.	Margaret Smith Court	1973
1377.	Monica Seles	1991
1378.	Ann Haydon Jones	1966
1379.	Nancy Richey	1968
1380.	Francoise Durr	1967

EXPERT - PAST MASTER - BORIS BECKER

1381.	Stefan Edberg
1382.	Ivan Lendl
1383.	4 (6-3, 6-7, 7-6, 6-4)
1384.	The French Open
1385.	3 (1987, 1989 & 1991)
1386.	1991 (January)

1387. 49
1388. Leiman
1389. The ATP World Tour Championship
1390. Andre Agassi

EXPERT - 2004 CHAMPIONS TOUR RANKINGS

1391.	Richard Krajicek	4th
1392.	Goran Ivanisevic	8th
1393.	Omar Camporese	13th
1394.	Petr Korda	Joint 16th
1395.	Paolo Cane	Joint 20th
1396.	Alex Antonitsch	Joint 16th
1397.	Cedric Pioline	Joint 20th
1398.	Emilio Sanchez	11th
1399.	Joao Cunha Silva	Joint 16th
1400.	Michael Stich	9th

EXPERT - 2003 CHAMPIONS TOUR RANKINGS

1401.	Michael Stich	3rd
1402.	Henri Leconte	5th
1403.	John McEnroe	1st
1404.	Pat Cash	17th
1405.	Cedric Pioline	Joint 11th
1406.	Thierry Champion	Joint 20th
1407.	Emilio Sanchez	Joint 13th
1408.	Yannick Noah	10th
1409.	Jeremy Bates	9th
1410.	Felip Dewulf	15th

EXPERT - WIMBLEDON RECORDS

1411. 33
1412. 49
1413. 12
1414. Elizabeth Ryan (7)
1415. K Davidson (AUS), K N Fletcher (AUS) & E V Seixas (USA)
1416. France
1417. Serena Williams (aged 16 in 1998)
1418. Martina Hingis (aged 15 in 1996)
1419. Martina Navratilova (aged 46 in 2003)
1420. Billie Jean King (1973)

EXPERT - WIMBLEDON LADIES DOUBLES WINNERS

1421.	Miss L M Raymond & Miss R P Stubbs	2001

1422.	Miss B C Fernandez & Miss N M Zvereva	1997
1423.	Miss J Novotna & Miss H Sukova	1990
1424.	Mrs G E Reid & Miss W M Turnbull	1978
1425.	Miss M Navratilova & Miss P Shriver	1981
1426.	Miss R Casals & Mrs L W King	1973
1427.	Miss A K Kiyomura & Miss K Sawamatsu	1975
1428.	Miss E F Goolagong & Miss M S A Michel	1974
1429.	Miss V E S Williams & Miss S J Williams	2000
1430.	Miss K Jordan & Miss A E Smith	1980

EXPERT - LEGEND - STEFFI GRAF

1431. 1987
1432. 1989, 1990 & 1992
1433. 1987, 1990 & 1994
1434. Lindsay Davenport (1999)
1435. 377
1436. 186
1437. 8
1438. 1987-1990 & 1993-1996
1439. The ITF World Championship
1440. 3 (gold in 1984 & 1988 and silver in 1992)

EXPERT - PAST MASTER - JOHN McENROE

1441. The French Open Mixed Doubles (with Mary Carillo in 1977)
1442. Jimmy Connors
1443. The Australian Open
1444. 4
1445. 1979, 1980, 1981 & 1984
1446. Peter Fleming
1447. 1979, 1981, 1983, 1984 (all with Peter Fleming) & 1992 (with Michael Stich)
1448. Tom Gullikson
1449. Ted James (Umpire) & Fred Hoyles (Referee)
1450. The French Open

EXPERT - LEGEND - CHRIS EVERT LLOYD

1451. 2
1452. 1982 & 1984
1453. 1974
1454. Evonne Cawley
1455. 1975, 1976, 1977, 1980 & 1981
1456. 18
1457. The Ladies' Singles at the 1986 French Open
1458. The US Open

1459. 53
1460. Evonne Goolagong Cawley

EXPERT - LEGEND - MARTINA NAVRATILOVA

1461. Zina Garrison
1462. 4 (1983, 1984, 1986 & 1987)
1463. 1982 & 1984
1464. Steffi Graf (1987, 1988 & 1989)
1465. 331
1466. 7 (1978-1979 & 1982-1986)
1467. Betty Stove
1468. The Mixed Doubles (with L Paes of India)
1469. 167
1470. 165

EXPERT - MIXED SETS - 1

1471. Boris Becker
1472. 1967
1473. Arthur Ashe
1474. J & T Austin (USA)
1475. Martina Navratilova (the Australian Open was not held in 1986)
1476. Cricket Club (Warehouseman's Cricket Ground in St Kilda, Melbourne)
1477. Zeljko Franulovic
1478. Maria Bueno
1479. John Newcombe & Tony Roche
1480. Evert - Chris (1) & Jeanne (9)

EXPERT - FACTS & TRIVIA

1481. Emilio & Javier Sanchez (Emilio won by 2 sets to 1)
1482. 6 (1981-1986)
1483. Bobby Riggs (she beat the ex-Wimbledon Champion 6-4, 6-3, 6-3)
1484. 1956
1485. Ilie Nastase
1486. Boris Becker
1487. Steffi Graf (4 Australian, 5 US Open, 6 French & 7 Wimbledon)
1488. Chris & Jeanne Evert
1489. Boris Becker (1985)
1490. Lleyton Hewitt & Lindsay Davenport

EXPERT - MIXED SETS - 2

1491. Martina Navratilova
1492. Julia Sampson (Australian) & Doris Hart (French, Wimbledon and US Open)
1493. Italian Championship

1494. Patrick Proisy
1495. US Open
1496. Billie Jean King & Martina Navratilova
1497. Alex Metreveli (3-0)
1498. John Bromwich (Australian), Roderick Menzel (French), Henry Austin (Wimbledon) & Gene Mako (US Open)
1499. Jana Novotna (1998)
1500. Ivan Lendl